HOW TO LAUNCH A SMALL BUSINESS

For Adventurers and Students

Allen M.Hans, Ph.D.

authorHOUSE®

AuthorHouse™
1663 Liberty Drive
Bloomington, IN 47403
www.authorhouse.com
Phone: 1-800-839-8640

First published by AuthorHouse 2/4/2010

ISBN: 978-1-4490-8134-8 (e)
ISBN: 978-1-4490-8133-1 (sc)

Library of Congress Control Number: 2010901109

Printed in the United States of America
Bloomington, Indiana

This book is printed on acid-free paper.

DEDICATION

To those who represent the future;
Nicole, Jacob, Gregory

PREFACE

The intent of this book is to provide the reader with the benefit of experiences learned during fifty years of participating in the growth and management of businesses.

Information and methods derived from these experiences provides a background for the adventurer and student who desire to explore the dynamics and techniques required for conducting a small business, and helps to provide direction toward reaching that objective.

People frequently think of a Small Business as being in the category of the proverbial Mom and Pop shop. Although such a small organization fits within the description of small business, they are not the definitive example.

A Small Business may include the following examples;

Sole Proprietorships, Corporations, Partnerships, Legal and Medical professional LLC's and Inc's, Trade associations/groups, Consultants, Software Designers, Accountants, Product Manufacturers, Service Enterprises, Plumbers, Contractors, Electricians, Auto Repair shops, Retail Sales organizations, Product or service distributors, Mom and Pop shops, Home businesses, etc. The list is extensive.

According to Wikipedia, "A small business is a business that is privately owned and operated, with a small number of employees, and relatively low volume of sales. Small businesses are normally privately owned corporations, partnerships, or sole proprietorships. The legal definition of "small" varies by country and by industry, but generally has fewer than 100 in the United States and under 50 employees in the European Union." Other counties define the number as low as enterprises with fifteen employees. (Figure A and B)

Part I, and Part II of the book compares the growth of *small business,* using *human growth* as an analogy or metaphor.

Part III, the largest part of the book, presents *lessons that life experiences in business* have taught.

The examples presented include both service and product business, encompassing a diverse market focus, and customer base.

So, turn the page and begin the voyage.

How To Launch A Small Business

For Adventurers and Students

Table of Contents

Part I-The Business Journey Begins

Introduction

"Business growth and human development are similar, understanding one helps to understand the other"

The person, who said that having and raising a family must be easy since everyone does it, is likely the same deranged person who said that all it takes to start a successful business and make lots of money is to have a good idea, develop the idea, produce it, and sell, sell, sell. I am here to tell you that this;"Just isn't so!"

This book will attempt to provide you with useful information in place of invalid common assumptions, and myths.

If being successful in business were so easy, life would provide the silver spoon to use when eating. As with most things, which look easy when done by the expert through trial and tribulation, success would appear guaranteed particularly for those who have not experienced it.

In reality, all it takes is *effort* in terms of hard work, obtaining *resources* in the form of financing, *support* through the hiring and paying employees, and *investment* of time and expenditure for suppliers, rent and utilities, and *survival* by enduring the rise and fall of sales and the whims of the marketplace.

Hey, wait a minute, these examples sound similar to the complexity of what is involved in the growth of a child, yes it does, and this book will demonstrate that *effort-resources-support* and *investment* are required to assure-*survival,* similarities that are vital to the growth of small business and the growth of a child.

So let us look at how the two compare, let us see what is behind the curtain, the story starts below.

CHAPTER 1- CONCEPTION

"There are intangibles that enter into the odds of success"

A journey is about to take place. With 6 billion people on this earth, it is not only possible but it is likely that at any time, somewhere, even if it is a 1 in 3 billion shot, that two people will meet. One may be the *idea person*, the other a *business kind of person* and they meet to discuss what it would take to start an *enterprise*. Thanks for statistical probability.

They will start the perilous trip from *idea* to *enterprise* in a manner similar to that of human development. If they succeed, there is a 50-50 chance that they will still be in business after five years. It does not sound like a slam-dunk, because it is not.

Do not get discouraged at this point because it frequently has a successful conclusion.

The road is similar in the human and business metaphor since both require arriving at important points along the route, intact and on time.

Just as all cells are at the start able to develop into specialized cells that perform specific functions during early human development. *Stem ideas* in the early development of business eventually morph in the *concept phase* to form the inputs of the *Business Plan*.

"The way it works, if successful"

If the fledgling embryonic development of the enterprise

is successful in generating a *business plan* that will result in an infusion of capital by investors, the project is thus *nourished* and may expand into the next stage of its development. In an emerging enterprise, it is the Business Plan that determines if the *organism* lives or dies.

Development

"Business uses a plan/roadmap with defined goals and resources"

Development is a continuous process and requires a road map or template as a guide down the path for results that are satisfactory.

Business *development* follows in a path toward independent operation as progress continues to achieve a viable product or service for the market. When a product or service is developed, it has to meet the *need* of the *end user* so that a *match* takes place between what is developed, and what is required by the market. Business *development* requires that it continually is robust. Each item must withstand the external environment associated with its utility or purpose therefore the identification of these requirements must be clearly defined and satisfied. The business encounters *harsh* environment changes from launch to the rigors of the marketplace.

Accomplishing tasks and reaching goals is only one part of the rules for starting a successful venture. Providing a product or service requires the coming together of the right resources in the right quantities at the right time. In particular, the parts and function of the *system/elements* must be clearly defined and evident.

Preparation for Launch

At *mission control,* the company founder and his staff sit at a conference table conducting its countdown to launch: Finances in place....check, Design completed....check, Testing completed...check, Pilot production underway... check, sales and marketing staff training completed... check, product orders received...check, material and supplies on hand...check. Preparation is completed and the company is ready to enter the market. The auspicious occasion is ready for celebration, as the company and the product are ready for launch. If the introduction is successful, the company is on its way...

Chapter 2- Growth Through Response To Stimulus

"Useful information can be obtained from history"

A number of observations made during the advancement of science by the ancient Greeks, Romans, and early Europeans paved the way to accumulation of scientific knowledge. This database of knowledge expands continually. Where as in the past, a *barber* would pull teeth or the local *shaman or witch docto*r would prescribe herbs, incantations and tonics to help people and animals survive disease and damage from attacks by predators. Today the *body of information* encompasses a huge number of *fact*s that provide the structure for business and professional practices.

"Facts, principles and motivation"

Information requires careful analysis prior to accepting the data as being *fact*. Data must meet the *test of logic-reason-rationality* and be based upon *sound and proven principles*. An enterprise that uses data to project the future needs to track actual results to validate those assumptions made. It is important that business *reach out* to potential customers to learn their needs and likes and dislikes. The motivation is to provide a product or service to the market, in the quantity and quality needed, thereby establish a sales base for repeat business. This is a major driving force that will determine success in business.

Chapter 3- Preparing For The Future

A. BUSINESS DEVELOPMENT

"A goal of business is to achieve a profit"

The goal of a business is to grow, develop, and *profit*. The objective is to act independently and responsibly based upon *self-interest* as motivation. Part of this process requires trial and error, and experiences in their unique environment.

"Plan for doing it properly"

Having achieved the first major step toward the goals of acceptance in the marketplace, the enterprise faces the challenge to establish a strategic and *tactical* plan that defines the direction, resources and methods required to meet the objectives. A strategic plan *focuses* on the marketing activity and needs to provide the roadmap towards reaching the sales projections, and the sales training and skills in order to market the product or service. A tactical plan needs to show *how to* implement the strategy developed and provide a definition of the tools, methods, and resources needed and to provide on time support in accomplishing the strategic requirements.

It is crucial that a customer base, or database, through which revenue is obtained, is established using data from sales activity involving the product or service.

Fits and *starts* are common, and the timing of events

in the supply chain requires a link to the demands of inventory or sales, but accomplishing this may not always occur on time.

In the case of services, the scheduling of customers or clients is important to optimize performance, but may not run smoothly due to unanticipated events. Contractors often encounter supply disruptions that may occur in delivery of materials needed, or weather conditions may delay the work.

These events is *expected* to occur since as with a growing child, the systems are being developed and exercised initially and not every target date will be immediately met.

"Anticipate what is required and respond"

An enterprise develops from a theoretical plan into an actual entity through implementation. Progress is measureable, to the requirements of the business plan, to assess if the activities are producing the required results.

The ability to anticipate, rather than respond by reflex to previous experience, is a process that develops over time when successful previous conditions and events have shown consistent results.

The rate of growth depends upon the abilities of the individuals who run the company. In small companies, communication between individuals is initially informal and may be very effective. It is important that response to customers and suppliers (if applicable) is communicated, timely, and thorough.

Achievement of results does not always occur with full control of the players, or totally by reasoned choice.

The *growth* plan takes place in concert with *capability*.

The variations in the type of business and field of enterprise require significant differences in approach. A McDonalds is different from a clothing store business, even though both offer products. Private school administration is different from an attorney's practice, even though both provide service.

"Monitor and understand when change is required"

Change is a normal part of growth and development. Factors such as changes in the market, which are outside the control of the company, often have direct impact on results. Measuring of progress will provide an opportunity to *correct course* in the use of resources and provide re-direction, if required.

B. THE TECHNOLOGY REVOLUTION

"Change brought about by technology"

Change in business and commerce during the 20th Century was dramatic, and never experienced to the same extent before this period.

"How things were"

A picture of life in the year 1900 in the United States would resemble the following: During evening, reading was from the light of lit candles or wicks saturated in kerosene. Horses and horse drawn carriages was the means of individual transportation (talk about pollution). Trains and boats were the method used for transporting people, food, clothing and durable goods, which were sold at local small shops.

Satisfying people's food wants and needs required a large number of small farms and ranches located across the country that produced less food using more resources than today.

Newspapers were the sole means of obtaining national or daily local information and news. People were limited in earning money due to inadequate training or education. Multigenerational families lived in the same house to support the family, and provide the manual labor required to perform the routine farming and household tasks.

"How things are now"

Contrast that with the year 2000 in the United States. Electric powered light and equipment, electric stoves, gas washers and dryers, automobiles to travel distant places, aircraft that are available to take hundreds of passengers all over the entire world in less than 48 hours travel time. Computers are available for writing documents, performing accounting functions and for storing information. The Internet is available for communicating with anyone or everyone that you know or wish to communicate with worldwide. Medical technology provides methods to detect illness through diagnostic equipment for internal scanning, blood testing for abnormalities and disease, surgical techniques to correct bone, muscle, organ, system defects and threats to health. Medical devices and biotechnology devices replace the critical functions of the body through life supporting and life sustaining technology.

Three major factors that have made the most important changes in business are; *innovation and technology, free trade through reduction of barriers, a free economy based upon capital investment leading to supply and demand economics.*

The result of creating simple methods for consumer product applications means that the user does not need to *understand* the technology to *use it.*

Chapter 4- The Formative Period

Survival and internal growth is critical. Most entities are subject to *rules* promulgated by outside sources such as Government Agencies, and many Professions impose rules associated with their specific interest or profession. This may create restriction and restraint to the way in which business carries out its function, often at the sacrifice of innovation and progress in the respective field or industry. However, it is important to protect the client or customer *safety* hence rules are required and valuable.

"Strength and weakness"

Companies display strengths and weakness regarding the attainment of goals and objectives. Since it is not possible to be all things to all people, product related companies select the *niche* or portion of a market to serve. In their environment, service industries and professional services choose the *specialty* where they are going to focus, their *niche* in the market.

Looking out from the inside
"Company Image"

A major factor in determining the *image* of the organization is the extent to which the leader takes an active role in guiding the policy and direction of the organization. The projected image of the organization is often provided by the sales or marketing function. It is important that agreement and harmony exists between the persons who interfaces with the customer and the principals of the enterprise.

Looking in from the outside
"The Customer view"

Customer satisfaction is a measure of progress of the organization. The purpose of enterprise is to satisfy a need in the marketplace either by supplying product or by providing service. Visits with customers, by members of management, are necessary to assure accuracy in the communication process. Participation in industry trade shows and professional conferences provides needed feedback. Participation at professional meetings and industry shows is a method to observe the effectiveness of communication, and if required, to take needed action to obtain the desired result. The attention to the customer, user, client and patient is a fundamental relationship that is the main factor in establishing and maintaining a successful enterprise, as it also is in interpersonal relationship throughout business and personal life.

Training and Skill Development
"People as resources"

In an enterprise, employees with previous experience constitute a large body of available talent. Through the application of apprenticeship and mentoring, individuals acquire the ability needed to perform specific tasks. Learning takes place both by formal procedural training using documented materials, and by repetition of the task under supervision in On-the-Job-Training. This development of employee skills, need to be an ongoing process in business. An organization's personnel are an excellent source of innovative and varied opportunity, to expand the knowledge base and culture. Invention and innovation is typically an unrestrained-freewheeling-creative activity, and should be encouraged and rewarded.

Chapter 5- The Integration and Expression Phase

There comes a time when the need for change in work area or specialization, and delegation of responsibility, in the organization becomes visible. This is particularly true with *small companies*. For example, when *do-it-all* personnel can no longer handle the magnitude or extent of the work, it often results in sub-standard accomplishment, rather than the *excellent* job done in the past. Many enterprises encounter this scenario at some point in their growth. A useful method to determine the existence of an issue is to periodically, ask an employee to describe their *job function*, what *projects* they are working on, the amount of *time* spent each week on each project, and to whom do they *report*. This inquiry will provide insight in making a judgment or required changes.

"As a company grows"

When an enterprise is experiencing rapid growth most individuals take on the scope of work required and a few individuals may be handling two, three, or even four functions.

When the enterprise has reached the point, where individuals can no longer perform multiple functions, it may be time to organize the enterprise along functional lines. For example establishing; a head of personnel, a head of engineering, a head of operations, etc., fundamental functions that support the nature of the enterprise. Although this model is usually helpful for manufacturing organizations, service and professional organizations may also encounter comparable issues with their business structure, which may require a realignment of the activities and functions.

It is common to see people leaving a company, and new people arriving at companies during this transition. It is important that in making changes, the leader of the enterprise choose the individuals who will support the existing organization and the new *approach* needed to advance the company's growth.

Applying acquired skills
"Expanding the business"

As an enterprise reviews its accomplishments, and weaknesses, it often is apparent that other opportunities exist which are within the scope of the organization. For example, a producer of a specific product, such as an appliance, may realize that an accessory for the product would enhance the nature of the product. Similarly, if the product is complex, such as a system, offering a service contract to the user may increase revenue and provide a more attractive and comprehensive package to the customer. This may also apply to the service provider as well. A plumber may be able to provide the customer with a maintenance contract for all plumbing needs such as for a plant watering system. A physician or other professional may establish a referral service for clients or patient needs, based upon professional experience, to help with related issues outside their immediate specialty.

Assessing competition and Risk
"The needs of the market"

Assessing competition is critical to the success of a business. Development of a marketing and sales program depends upon the expectation of how well the product or service measures up with the competition. In marketing, there are basically two types or markets; one that already exists where product or service is currently in supply hence the plan is to garner market share, the other scenario is to develop a market for a product or service where no supply currently exists. The enterprises future may depend upon how well the results of this analysis meet the expectations of the market. The service provider similarly has the task of determining the *market* and in which manner the service will satisfy the need of the clients.

For example, a physician may have a specialized practice in a particular discipline and set up their practice in a specific location, which may or may not be optimal or viable in that area, whereas setting up in a different location may be appropriate.

Roles and rules
"How the business functions"

The formalization of the rules and responsibilities of the business enables the employees to understand their roles in the working of the enterprise. It also provides a means for evaluating performance and rewarding accomplishment.

There reaches a point, in most organizations, where there is a need to formalize methods and procedures to operate the company in an efficient manner. It is necessary that working plans be in place and functioning to increase efficiency, and the resulting profit derived through achieving a suitable level of control of process, costs, and efficiency.

Defining of roles for each functional activity is initially an issue for some employees in some enterprises. The view that the *old and informal* way of doing things *are good enough* may be a way for dealing with the need for formalization, by some of the employees who may view change as a reduction in job freedom and flexibility. They may also be concerned that the structuring of the rules and roles may diminish their personal importance in the organization.

CHAPTER 6- STEADY GROWTH

"The future"

A period of steady growth presents an opportunity for the company to take stock of where it has been, where it is and where it is going in the future. Professionals engaged in service activities, such as MDs, Lawyers, Accountants, etc., might benefit from using this opportunity to establish and develop partnerships or business collaborations.

Product producers may look at strategic acquisitions, off shore or outsource suppliers, in house production under private labeling, etc. to form a panorama of available improvements in technology.

These activities continue to *stay the course* when growth is adequate and consistent. Opportunities occur to improve the organization, through the training of people and by further developing their skills to expand their usefulness and functional capability, such as with cross training.

Chapter 7- Quantum Leap- A Change Of State

"Adolescence"

The gathering storm may begin as a sense of restlessness as a sense of discontent regarding the organizations growth and development. The *company management* may see the need to do things differently and make changes in the way it does business. This realization is a beginning of the *adolescence period* for the organization.

It is an opportunity to streamline and focus on conducting the business in a more efficient and effective way to improve its share of the market and provide for growth in personnel development.

The enterprise may need additional capital to finance the reaching of current or new goals and objectives. Through going public for obtaining funds for growth, for example, the enterprise may finance expansion and product diversification. However, the company must take on additional responsibility and cost when seeking this method to pursue growth.

Dynamic Evolution versus Chaotic Revolution "The rational versus the irrational"

Two kinds of behavior and growth may take place during this period, evolution, or revolution. Evolutionary change requires time and plan whereas revolutionary change is typically chaotic and involves both drastic action and expenditure of large amounts of energy and resources.

Recognizing the need to meet challenge in the marketplace may require a significant change in the way of doing business. To achieve this objective for expanding into new markets or accomplish major change in existing product, to make it more attractive to the customer, requires investigation and investment of time and financial resources

The acquisition of another company in the field or through collaboration with other companies, to obtain financing for the development of new product, or to obtain the resources for accomplishing changes of product line, is a major effort and requires considerable and careful analysis, discussion and planning.

Control
"Focusing energy"

During any transition, the enterprise must take the responsibility for initiating action and conducting the required activities. The result of outside influence exercised by the market, regulatory requirements, the financial environment, and *force majeure* affect the business outcome.

The transition from a small young organization, toward meeting the needs of a larger more mature organization, ultimately will result in a different structure, and scope of the business.

The choices made during this process *will* involve questions of organizational structure, redefining objectives the organization needs to pursue, considering strategic alliances, product lines, new product development, outsourcing manufacturing.

For service organizations, and professional service-providers a similar process of exploration becomes an important consideration, which utilizes both energy and time.

Challenge
"Ideas versus Action"

Organizations face challenges regarding acceptance in the *outer* world. An internal review of the organization may lead to realizing the difference between the creative *inventor-entrepreneurial* and the structured *business manager* way of thinking. The challenge is in preserving the inventor-entrepreneurial creativity needed for new product and marketing, while expanding the business-manager role within the organization structure and influence. This is often a challenging effort. The culture of the company evolves though growth from a young company to a more mature organization. This process of self-discovery is complex and may not yield immediate answers. At some point in time, the establishment will need to reassess future goals and objectives and the plan to achieve them.

Quantum change
"The level of growth"

Initially, enterprises go through changes considered *incremental* changes. Whereas, many companies see themselves as still just *a larger-small* company as they grow into becoming a mature business, in fact such is not the case. The development from a young to a more mature company is often not a *transition* it is a major event. Movement toward this objective may take place over a short period, as a *change of state*, and have a profound impact on the business hence it would be a *quantum* change.

During this process, the enterprise will have made decisions concerning hiring professional talent. Those in leadership roles in the company may have reached the point where they may not be capable of taking the company to the next step required. Those who possess the required skill *set* will be required to formulate and implement both policy and plan to take the company forward.

Integration and Self Control of Destiny "Reaching the goal"

As the enterprise reaches the stage of development where it prepares to take on the challenges that the business's future requires, the organization will have demonstrated that it can encounter and resolved issues and problems.

Future growth of the business often requires outside support services that provide fundamental research, or research and creative development, as the company moves forward

Manufacturing businesses that compete in technology products, or the expansion or growth industries, are motivated to achieve through their own creativity and independence.

Market driven ventures differ from enterprises that derive their income from government contracts or state or local support which depend upon those forces for determining their growth and sustenance tend to be less independent in action and path. It is true with individuals and organizations that choosing direction requires independence.

Now let us look at the growth of a human and see how it compares

Part II-The Human Journey Begins

Introduction

Let us now examine the trials and tribulations involved in raising a family, it starts simply enough, having sex and then nurturing and teaching the little rascal how to get through the hurts and dangers of growing up so that they and you eventually reach success and the *"promised land"*.

The progeny is now eighteen years old. You think they are old enough to be responsible for their own life, only to find out that the end is not yet there. There is college, financial support, housing, and the myriad of real life experiences that form a part of early adulthood that they are so eager to *share* with you. If all goes well eventually you, and they, reach the objective of independence.

Hey, wait a minute this sounds similar to what is involved in starting a business (*effort-resources-support* and *investment* are required to assure-*survival)*. It does, and this section of the book will demonstrate that these similarities are valid.

Chapter 8- Human Conception

"The start"

It may seem *fateful* when one in a million sperm joins with an egg to form a Human embryo. In *life,* you start the *game* and then take your *chances,* as they come.

This story starts when the egg and sperm meet on the fallopian tube subway. The trip is rapid and fraught with dangerous twists and turns. The express train stops as the embryo reaches the Uterus. If it is still on track, the embryo fastens to the soft luscious uterine wall and the process of growth and development takes place for an interminable 9 months of maternal host's discomfort.

Not all journeys go to the end of the line, but the odds are in favor of a successful launch. The transition from a self-sufficient embryo to fetus is a 'truth test' and determines if all conditions are correct so that development may continue.

CHAPTER 9- VIABILITY

"The human plan compared to the business plan"

Now that we have gotten past the *mechanics* of conception and the successful attachment of the embryo to the nourishing *hosts'* Uterus, let us look at the next step along the journey.

All the cells in the embryo-fetus are now multiplying, not in a haphazard way, but according to plan. What plan you ask? The DNA/RNA plan for *life* present in all living matter. Chromosomes and their genes contain preprogrammed instructions, just as the *business plan* says how to develop the business, along specific routes. The objective in raising a child is to reach *maturity* as the result of growth and development.

Design
"The blueprint for human growth"

Development is continuous and requires a road map or template as a guide down the path of growth for the results to be satisfactory. There is a way to make sure that the correct implementation of the systems and functions occur along the way. This takes place as the form and function of each of the parts is established, and organic systems developed for functionality are tested. Realizing that an Ape and Human share over 97% of the same genetic code explains a lot about our soon to become infant's behavior!

The birth of a viable infant requires the coming together of the right resources in the right quantities at the right times and prepares the infant to withstand the *harsh* environment changes as the infant experiences the drama of birth and the future.

Preparation for Launch

Mission Control is conducting the countdown. The final checklist is taking place, to make sure that the mission is a 'go' and not 'aborted'. Lets listen in on the conversation; Heart pumping...check, Brain engaged...check, Sensors for sound-sight-touch-connected and functioning.... check. The capsule with its precious cargo encased inside the launch vessel is on the launch platform inside the silo. The precious cargo attached to a tether/umbilical cord, for fuel, energy and waste disposal is preparing to take over these vital functions. The countdown continues. Motion sensors operating....check, fuel level ...check. As the team prepares for launch continues a heightened sense of expectation occur at mission control. The crew has completed its checklist and now the moment that all has been waiting for...birth. The muscles are contracted in a spasmodic rhythm the launch is underway. The capsule slowly emerges from the silo. As it enters the outside world, the fetus takes-over its own control, as it emerges as an infant. As the tether is severed, that has connected it to its mother; the infant takes its first breath. It is on the path toward childhood and beyond.... (Fig. D).

Chapter 10- Growth Through Response To Stimulus

"Addressing fundamental needs"

The infant responds to *hard wired* needs to seek out the source of nourishment. When it finds it, it reacts with a total response easily observed. This is a simple method for it to respond. *Stimulus-Action-Results*

Infants develop a database of information as they respond repeatedly to internal and external stimulus. Appropriate response to stimulus reinforces the lesson.

Combining thinking with action, such as in smiling and cooing is part of a *feedback loop* that provides quick learning and response in an efficient system.

The newborn is in constant motion during waking hours. Their hands and feet are moving almost nonstop. Their eyes attempt to track external motion in their view, their head moves toward sound, and their mouth and tongue are in motion ready to respond to their hunger signal. Initially, the infant is only concerned with satisfying their inborn needs, food, sleep, comfort. Soon as the infant starts to observe the external world, they observe images and sounds, and experiences life, with curiosity. The motivation is to satisfy essential needs.

Chapter 11- Transition

"Nature and nurture"

The brain develops using both internal and external stimulus. Part of this process requires trial and error. The child experiences their environment in a unique manner that continues throughout life. The infant develops and progresses through little changes, as it recognizes their reality that takes place repeatedly along the road to achievement. Genetic factors are expressed in concert with the nurturing that the child receives

Activity and achievement is a natural part of individual motivation toward maturity. This process involves learning from mistakes and seeing life in the broader context by relying on one's own resources to resolve problems and challenges that come up in everyday life, just as a business encounters.

CHAPTER 12- THE CONNECTION

"Reflex compared with learned response"

The journey throughout human history involved developing tools necessary for survival and through response of the primitive brain functions. The *flight or fight* reflex is an instinctive response to danger. When confronted with an imminent attack by a large carnivore our ancestors had to immediately respond, or risk being dinner for a saber tooth tiger and literally becoming history. Correct instinctive reflective behavior is proof of the ability to manage risk, which is an integral part of a successful life. When an infant hears a loud noise, it responds with the *startle reflex* or response. As it develops the responses to noise and other distractions, inputs from the higher cognitive brain functions determine the appropriate measured and reasoned act.

Having achieved the first major step toward adulthood, by surviving the rigors of gestation and birth, the infant embarks on the journey toward self-discovery and realization and self-accomplishment.

The next step along the journey involves acquiring skills to move actively and processes information, which we recognize as learning. The infant may experience what he hears as a lot of gibberish but shortly it has acquired the ability to recognize language and put forth effort associated with the learning process. Physical growth includes muscles for locomotion and vocalization, as well as mental development. The infant may be like a twenty-pound *gorilla*, full of energy and activity, not always self directed or carrying out movements with full control of physical dexterity or reasoned choice.

This too is evident in small business during the early years.

A desire to walk may be for naught if the muscles are not ready to support its weight and the neurological/ brain pathway developed.

These events are consistent between societies, cultures and races so that the events and timing of occurrence can be cataloged and serve as a method of determining normal growth parameters as for height and weight. (Figure C).

Change is the normal condition, and differences resulting from changes extend to the entire realm of human existence from the individual to societies and culture, and to business.

We often associate change with improvement but in reality, change may result in events that are *better or worse*. The only valid conclusion is that *status quo* no longer exists, even though we tend to focus on a return to *normalcy*, we tend to pay more attention to the exception, not the rule.

Chapter 13- The Formative Years

"The growth process"

Growth and development of the individual's potential is difficult to measure in absolute terms. It is more likely that observed deficiencies may result in lack of achieving full potential due to genetics that often affect outcome and achievement. One should not rush to judgment, in this mater. Albert Einstein did not speak until well past the normally expected age for speaking. Other individuals reach thresholds for physical and emotional accomplishment at either earlier or later dates than the norm, the child will grow and develop at their own schedule (Figure C). So does business.

Looking out from the inside reveals a number of observable factors that illustrate the perspective that a child has regarding its surroundings. The child develops recognition of the positive impact that its words and actions may have upon its acceptance and derived pleasure, or the effect that negative reaction to its words or action, by others, has upon its sense of well being.

The learning process consists of both the transfer of skills that take place informally as well as formal training. Children exhibit enthusiasm toward achieving satisfaction of accomplishment. *Trying* is not an end-point; *accomplishment* is the reward for effort and achievement of goals. Children typically have a short attention span, unless the task or activity itself provides the motivation for continuing, as evidenced by computer games that often occupy hours of interest.

The acquisition of knowledge and skill development, have a common denominator, interest. The child learns through both imitating an adult, or older child, and by repetition of the subject to be learned, or motivated by involvement in shared interest

Chapter 14- The Integration and Expression Phase

"Conflicting choices"

The child has learned a number of skills necessary for transition from an outside-dependent child, to self-dependent. In those major areas of life, the child can do many of the *routine* functions needed to satisfy its primary needs. There are conflicting needs between "I can do it myself" versus the need for you to do it for them. The child looks toward the outside world through involvement with a parent, or others that deals in *the outside* world of the child.

There is more developed expansion of language utilizing various forms of writing and extended reading containing factual events and people. This introduces the child to conceptual materials, such as, those involving mathematical principles and scientific formulation, historical perspective and the arts. Such is also the formula for developing leadership in business.

CHAPTER 15- STEADY GROWTH

The security of the home environment and subsequent tranquility in the child's life during the start of the second decade of childhood permits steady and consistent growth. The child pursues opportunities to reach out to fulfill their needs and wants. It explores improving relationships, as well as attempting new activities, and exercising greater mobility by traveling distances in expanding their world by exploration.

The child approaches the end of childhood and is about to enter the age of *adolescence*. Preadolescence is a time of change in the landscape. Reinforcement of rules and roles occur along with a sense of expectation and uncertainty, and developing a number of skill and achievements make it possible for them to take upon greater responsibility.

CHAPTER 16- QUANTUM LEAP-A CHANGE OF STATE

The gathering storm may begin as a sense of restlessness, discontent, irritability, on the part of the child, but begin, it will. Around the ages of 11 to13 years old, the child's world enters into a state of flux, fueled by hormonal activity that result in accelerated growth and gender appropriate changes, as well as other physical, mental and emotional change. Adolescence is *the* major time of *change* in the individual. It is the transition from child to adult and from childlike dependency, for satisfying needs, on others to a maturity that entails self-confidence and acceptance of responsibility as well as acting through independent action. It requires changes in physical, mental and emotional response to others.

"Adolescence to maturity"

During adolescence, change may take place with two kinds of behavior and growth; evolution, or revolution. The change due to evolution requires both time and exercising limited control. Change through revolution is typically chaotic and involves both drastic action and expenditure of large amount of energy and resources. The adolescent is often ambivalent, and the movement from child to adult does not take place as a straight-line function nor is it a smooth transition. This period of *change* is a period of *fits* and *starts*, attempts and accomplishment, success and failure. It is a continual challenge between agreement and antagonism, challenge and acceptance, assertion and acquiescence.

Growth requires dealing with two types of control: internal, and external. Adult behavior requires full control of the internal self, as well as exerting limited control in effecting results by externally controlled activity. Movement toward an objective requires energy and the teenager utilizes a significant amount of energy for the process of physical and metal growth.

The awareness of the scope and depth of discovery takes time and requires introspection through evaluating the outside world. The question is how does the person relate and how does one establish and satisfy its own future goals and objectives.

The transition in business from a small starting enterprise to that of a self-confident success in the market is analogous to human growth during this period.

Change from a child to adult is viewed as an incremental step by step process that take place over a number of years, and is often seen as a gradual process continual process (Figure C) . Mental and emotional change may be considered as a *quantum change*, in that the adult is not a *bigger child* but is in reality an adult a significantly different person altogether.

PART III- LESSONS FROM LIFE EXPERIENCES

CHAPTER 17- THE CHALLENGES OF OPERATING A BUSINESS

Parts 1 and II of this book employed the growth and development of a human organism, as a metaphor to describe the stages in the growth and development of small business.

This, Part III, will explore the lessons learned during fifty years in businesses in the United States, and Internationally with companies of from five to five hundred employees. During which time, I have had the pleasure of participating in three careers; as an employee in three state-of-the art technology companies, owner of a consultancy, and teacher and lecturer.

"Background"

Beginning with the 1950's, employment opportunities became available in a number of companies dealing in *state of the art* high-technology products. These included positions in engineering and production for a Defense Contractor, employment in R&D and manufacturing in the emerging Semiconductor industry followed by employment in the Aerospace solar cell and solar panel industry. Focus and opportunities then shifted to employment in the new field of Medical devices with an opportunity to join companies producing implantable medical devices, and patient monitoring systems.

Interest in starting a business venture, was realized with the establishment of a Management Consultancy, which has been serving companies for over the past twenty-three years.

Education and professional development, obtained through over 50 years of experience participating in science and industry, has provided a background that has proven beneficial to clients of the consulting venture.

Teaching a course in a post-graduate university level program, and in addition technology and motivational speaking engagements, have rounded out this adventure.

It is a privilege, to share with you, the accumulated knowledge and experience derived from these adventures.

Chapter 18- Planning Business Development

Planning a business involves six (6) steps, in accomplishing the development of the enterprise, as follows:

1-Determine a **Philosophy**
2-Identify the **Principles**
3-Establish a **Policy**
4-Generate a **Plan**
5-**Execute** the Plan
6-Follow through to reach **Achievement**

Accomplishing these steps provides direction and substance toward your quest for business excellence. The following chapters will permit you the visibility and detail to put you on the road to success.

Establishing a Business Philosophy

A *Mission Statement* establishes a clear set of rules and objectives that management expects the organization to strive for in their dealings both within the organization and in interfacing with the outside world. A mission statement expresses management's commitment to conduct the business, to reflect the objectives it believes are appropriate in its dealing with employees and customers.

The nature of business is to serve the customer/user/client/patient. The aim is to provide product or service at a price that both agree upon in accordance with a code of ethics, rules of conduct, and by the informal rules of the game. Legal rules and regulation apply where product or service is available to the public, and where public trust may be affected, or where life or limb may be at risk.

In situations where there are no specified terms or conditions associated with the provision of goods or services, there are implied conditions relating to the good or service provided. For example, when a person buys product at a retail store or produce at the local food market, there is an implied expectation of *usability,* that is, the item will meet with the stated function or features promised to the buyer/user. Often there is an *implied* understanding that there is a *reasonable* expectation of satisfying the user. Any dissatisfaction requires resolution by the seller or provider, without question of legal proof. Who is going to challenge a person who purchases produce, and did not find the fruit acceptable?

In the realm of service providers, the *subjective* evaluation by the client/patient provides latitude in determining acceptance. Since service is frequently provided, and warranted, on a *best efforts* basis there is opportunity for negotiating compliance criteria.

The professional's degree of competence is frequently measured by formal education and previous experience, and those imposed by regulatory bodies. That provides a basis for the choice from which a customer/user/patient/client may make a decision, when seeking the specific service. This applies to professional services which include lawyers, physicians, dentists, plumbers, electricians, accountants, financial planners, automobile mechanics, physical therapists just to name a few.

It is often necessary to establish and provide a business

philosophy beyond those required by legal or regulatory entities. The statement of a business philosophy may be contained in a *Mission Statement*, a *Quality Policy Statement* or a *Statement of Ethical Principles* expressed in broad terms, or by an accepted creed such as the *Hippocratic Oath*.

MISSION STATEMENTS

An example of a mission statement for a retail business:

American Baking Company strives in all words and action;
To create a fun, supportive and fair work environment,
To provide friendly, personal services to our customer,
To ensure the highest standards of product quality,
To be fair, honest and considerate in our relationship with our suppliers,
To be the best Bakery in America!.

An example of a mission statement for a manufacturer:

"It is the objective of ABC Incorporated to achieve excellence. It is our commitment to provide; the best value to our customers and users through perseverance and the demonstration of sound business practice, to strive for always pursing excellence, and by establishing and monitoring achievement of our goals, and by conscientiously translating the latest technology of our industry to create an ever increasing value to our customers.

We are committed to pursuing new customers by: motivating our team through training and incentive programs, conducting monthly business development meetings with our associates, to meet both our commitment to customers and commitment to the investors and

> *stakeholders of our company, by increasing revenue through implementing and developing continuously improved product and service."*

Identifying business principles

Application of business principles is essential in serving the customer. It is this interface between the company and the customer, which determine a sale.

In establishing an approach to meet the needs and wants of the customer, the business's agent must understand just what the company stands for and what its principles are, so that the business dealings reflect a correct message.

Success or failure of an enterprise rests on the ability to both attract capable sales talent as well as training the sales people on the policy and methods concerning *total customer service.* Customer service is establishing a relationship with the customer where the customer acknowledges receipt of a fair deal, and a continuing commitment by the company to the customer to resolve any issues that may occur regarding product or service.

Entities that provide primarily a service or function of a vocational or professional nature, requires an understanding of the extent that sales plays in meeting the customer/client/patient/user requirements. Service suppliers may not always receive direct *feedback* regarding customer satisfaction. For example, when an auto is brought into a service shop due to a noise, as long as the noise is no longer heard when the car is driven away from the shop, the customer is satisfied. This does not necessarily mean that the service person eliminated the noise by fixing the original *problem* that caused the noise.

A measure of customer satisfaction is, when a customer returns for other additional service.

Beyond legal obligations, the conduct of business reflects upon an enterprise in other ways. The reputation a company earns is a *value* measured when a company is growing, or when transacting a sale of the business. It is a value called *good will*. The question of the *fairness* of a transaction in free trade is a *win-win* situation where both the buyer and seller are willing to execute the exchange of goods or service, for perceived value.

Providing product or service is either; self-regulated, or subject to enforced regulation. The difference between the two choices is a matter of both the market and the industry/profession. In a self-regulated condition, the marketplace provides a critical role in assuring that the enterprise, conducts business in an ethical manner. Two forces accomplish this effect; *competition* and *word of mouth or reputation,* which may be favorable or unfavorable comments about the practices of an enterprise. Current and former employees and contractors weigh in on the conduct of the enterprise. In some industries, there are independent third parties such as Consumer Union, Good Housekeeping, the Better Business Bureau or Chambers of Commerce that provide visibility to potential and actual clients or customers. In a regulated field or industry, the conduct of an enterprise is subject to both civil litigation and criminal action through the court system and through the news media and on *blogs* and other internet sites.

Perhaps the most significant measure of the integrity and honesty of an organization is how the employees are treated. Those companies that provide a healthy growing environment, with all employees equally treated with courtesy, respect and value, also tend to act toward their customers in the same way

BUSINESS PRINCIPLES

The primary goal of XYZ Corporation shall be to achieve the highest quality in processes, products and services. Attainment of this goal shall be foremost in all business methods and practices. It shall serve as the principal criterion guiding design, development, manufacture and distribution of our products and services for the express purpose of always exceeding customer expectations and complying with the requirements of all applicable regulatory agencies, around the world

Management remains committed to the creation of an environment that consistently fosters employee understanding of quality as our guiding principle. Our company communicates this goal through action, example and formal employee education. It is our aim to train, facilitate and motivate all employees, actively participate in the process of continuous quality improvement.

Establishing Business Policy

A business policy compliments the commitment to the business principles. The business policy reflects the dealings within the organization. Achieving a meaningful business policy requires that the business management carefully considers how to implement the company's principles in order to conduct the day to day business that is encountered in conduct of staff and others who represent the business owners interest.

The business policy needs to state in clear terms understandable by the people who will utilize the policy to interface both, within the organization and the *outside world.* It may contain the company's desires in the realm of quality, service, regulatory or regulation requirements, etc. It also identifies the basic description of the methods for complying with external requirements. For example, the policy demonstrates the company commitment to training employees in *quality* matters as well as communicating with the organization the *goals and objectives* that management intends to achieve. It is the statement of *intent* regarding a *code of behavior* and action regarding responsibilities both legal and civil. It is a statement to customers/clients/users/patients regarding the commitment of the organization to achieving its moral and ethical objectives.

BUSINESS POLICY

It is ABC Incorporated business policy to engage in the highest ethical and moral principles in our interface with employees, suppliers, stakeholders, and customers. We ascribe to a firm principle of fundamental mutual respect toward all relationships that we enter into. We have established program and training designed to achieve, self-imposed requirements, requirements of the marketplace and those requirements imposed upon our company and people by regulation in our field of endeavor.

It is our goal, intent, and desire, to effectively, and completely achieve this policy in principle and action and to seek confirmation of achievement by feedback and input from all participants as we strive toward continuous improvements in our efforts and accomplishments.

Generating the Business Plan

The business plan is a plan of anticipation. It is a, prediction (*pro forma*) of events and outcomes for establishing, growing, and maintaining the health and profitability of the enterprise.

A business plan requires that both tangible as well as intangible factors that can or will happen, that affect the potential and actual happenings in the establishment and conduct of the business, be defined and evaluated. It addresses a number of phases and steps in the business life. Starting with the inception of the business and continuing with the developing of the business model, the plan extends the timeframe from the immediate to the future. In some business plans the expectations for the business during the first two or three years is detailed. In other plans, dependent upon the nature of the enterprise, it may include focus on R&D activities. In still other plans emphasis is given to specific cost factors and timing of events when additional resources may be needed.

BUSINESS PLAN

An effective business plan will help provide visibility to both the company and potential investors. The plan as a minimum contains the following:

1. 'Executive Summary'. The summary outlines the goals and objectives as a business strategy. It is important for communicating to employees and potential customers what your ideas are.

2. 'History'. This is the story of creation of the company. It is how the principles came up with the idea to start the business.

3. State the Company goals and objectives. Describe your short- and long-term goals and objectives for the company and the timing of growth. Identify who will be your primary customers.

4. Describe the management team. *Include the names and backgrounds of key members of the management team and their respective responsibilities.*

5. Describe the service or product that you plan to offer. *Clearly describe how your product or service differs from everything else on the market.*

6. Analyze the market potential for the service or product that you will offer. *Be convincing in explaining why the market you are after is relatively large and growing. Conduct research for this section and determine the base of your business. Business may be local, on the Internet or provide product or services to other market environments.*

7. Provide a marketing strategy. *A plan for telling the world you are open for business. Identify if you will rely exclusively on word of mouth, advertising in print, on television or on the Web or a combination of all three. It is important to identify how much you plan to spend on marketing.*

8. Provide a statement of the three to five year business financial projections. *Identify your financial forecasts, with spreadsheets showing the formula you used to reach your projections. Provide balance sheets, income statements and cash-flow projections for the entire forecast period. Summarize how much money you would like to borrow to cover your startup costs. The assumptions that you make in this section will make or break your company's success. It may be worth obtaining outside support in generating the financial modeling needed.*

9. Generate an exit strategy. *Lay out the benchmarks that may be required in deciding to exit the business. This strategy based upon a dollar figure, revenue growth, the market's reception to your idea, or a consensus among top officers.*

Executing the Plan

The business plan contains the template for the growth and development of the business. The plan also states the events and the timeframe for accomplishing activities that are required and a schedule for completion. It also defines the resources, including the staff required, and a schedule for funds, and endpoints. It must define the steps required, and estimate of the likelihood of achieving the anticipated end-results. Dependence on outside sources and availability of critical elements to achieve results need to be addressed. A sales plan contains an estimate of sales volume and price that are factors in the plan. An analysis of product, and need, availability is essential in determining the pricing and volume expected at each point in the timeline.

Companies come in different sizes, shapes, and mixes. The plan requires analysis of the business with respect to these variables.

There are three primarily small product manufacturing business models, these are as follows; a) Low cost, high volume product, simple technology, sold through distributors, b) Moderate cost, volume product, moderate technology, sold through sales representatives or an in house sales force, c) High cost, low volume product, high technology, sold through wholesalers or an in house sales force. There are *significant* variations of these basic business models for example products may be marketed through agents, representatives, through distributors, company direct sales, company or outside phone sales, and independent sales organizations to name a few sales structures. Sales volume and level of technology may also vary within this model structure

A major factor in setting up and executing the plan is an analysis of the most effective sales model. In analyzing the costs of sales, it is necessary that there is an understanding of what constitutes the selling price and what will be required to assure that the sales-organization may achieve their goals. In a high volume production manufacturing case, it is important to realize that when selling through a distribution chain, a small change in unit price to the distributor may reflect a large dollar amount per year due to the high volume involved. In the sale of low volume products, a small incremental pricing may not significantly affect profitability. Other costs result in significant price change, such as with a complex product where installation, shipping, and service are major factors in the final cost of the product/system. The price determination has to include the accounting and financial factors in determining the costs as well as the requirements for payables and how that will have an effect on cash outflow

FINANCIAL STATEMENTS

Financial statements provide an overview of a business or person's financial condition in both short and long term. All the relevant financial information of a business enterprise, presented in a structured manner and in a form easy to understand, called the financial statements. There are four basic financial statements:

*1. **Balance sheet** referred to as statement of financial position or condition, reports on a company's assets, liabilities, and net equity as of a given point in time.*

*2. **Income statement** also referred to as Profit and Loss statement ("P&L"), reports on a company's income, expenses, and profits, over time. Profit & Loss account*

provide information on the operation of the enterprise. These include sale and the various expenses incurred during the processing state.

3. Statement of retained earnings *explains the changes in a company's retained earnings over the reporting period.*

4. Statement of cash flows *reports on a company's cash flow activities, particularly operating, investing and financing activities.*

For larger corporations, these statements are often complex and may include an extensive set of notes to the financial statements and management discussion and analysis. The notes typically describe each item on the balance sheet, income statement and cash flow statement in further detail. Notes to the financial statement, are an integral part of the financial statements.

Balance Sheet
Date_____

Assets		Liabilities & Equity	
CURRENT ASSETS	**x100**	**CURRENT LIABILITIES**	**x100**
Cash in Banks	$1000	Notes Payable-To Banks	$ 3500
Cash on Hand	$2000	Notes Payable-To Trade	$1000
TOTAL CASH	**$3000**	Notes Payable-To Other	$ 500
RECEIVABLES		Accounts Payable	$2500
Notes-Trade	$5000	Loan on Life Insurance	$ 0
Notes-Other	$1000	Due to Officer, Partners,.	$ 0
Accounts-Other	$ 300	Income Taxes Payable	$ 150
Less Debt Reserves	$ 0	Other Taxes Payable	$ 0
		Salaries & Wages Accrued	$ 600
Total Receivables-	**$9,500**	Position of Long Term Debt	$ 100
		TOTAL CURRENT LIABILITIES	**$ 8,350**
INVENTORY			
Finished Merchandise	$ 1500	**LONG TERM LIABILITIES**	
Work in Process	$ 3000	Bonded Debt	$ 0
Raw Materials	$5000	Mortgages & Leans Payable	$30000
Supplies	$1000	Notes-Long Term	$ 4500
Other	$ 500	Less Current Position	$ 0
TOTAL INVENTORY	**$11,000**	**TOTAL L-T LIABILITY**	**$34,150**
Life Insurance Surrender Value	$1000		

Government Security	$ 250			
Other Marketable Securities	$ 50			
Other Current Assets	$ 0			
TOTAL CURRENT ASSETS	***$21,800***			
FIXED ASSETS				
Land	$10000			
Buildings	$25000			
Machinery & Equipment	$ 5000			
Vehicles	$ 2500			
OTHER FIXED ASSETS				
Define	$ 0			
Sub Total				
Less Accumulated	($ 0)			
TOTAL ASSETS	***$42,500***	***TOTAL LIABILITIES***	***$42,500***	

PROFIT AND LOSS STATEMENT

January 1, 2005 through December 31, 2005

INCOME
Income	$200,000
Total Income	$200,000

Expense
Accounting	$ 3,500
Marketing & Ads	$105,000
Taxes	$ 57,000
Telephone	$ 4,800
Total Expense	$170,300

NET INCOME $ 29,700

RETAINED EARNINGS (IN A BALANCE SHEET)

Assets		Liabilities & Owner Equity	
Cash	$ 6,600	Notes Payable	$ 0
Accounts Receivable	$ 6,200	Accounts Payable	$ 30,000
		Total Liabilities	$ 30,000
Tools & Equip	$25,000	Owner's Equity	
		Capital Stock	$ 7,000
		Retained Earnings	$ 800
		Total Owners Equity	$ 7,800
TOTAL	$ 37,800	TOTAL	$ 37,800

CASH FLOW

Statement of Cash Flow for the period
01/01/2006 to 12/31/2006

Cash flow from operations	*$ 4,000*
Cash flow from investing	*$(1,000)*
Cash flow from financing	*$(2,000)*
NET INCREASE (decrease) in cash	***$1,000***

Achieving Results

Effective and timely implementation of the business plan is crucial. Communication feedback is required in real time, in order to achieve the required results. Delays are common when unexpected events occur, and needed resources are not on time. A clear understanding of the cause and the corrections for issues are required and are included in the plan. A significant error often made in business plans and their execution, this is, *over optimistic projections*. In reality, unexpected events do happen. A *contingency plan* must be a part of the implementation expectation. The contingency plan should address each element and provide three models; a schedule that is an *optimistic* schedule, a *pessimistic* schedule, and a *planned* schedule based upon anticipation of elements and events happening on time.

IMPLEMENTATION PLAN

PLAN

_Issues to Be Resolved

* Expansion of rooms and doors for production areas
* Assure enough maintenance parts are on order
* Secure enough marking materials
* Obtain sufficient packaging boxes
* Establish material requirement database for raw materials
*Test the equipment for proper operation

SCHEDULE

1. Define product operations by March 25
2. Select and purchase equipment by March 26
3. Discuss employee functions with leaders by March 28
4. Hire ten (10) employees by April 07
5 Train the four inspectors and six production operators by April 12
6. Complete the installation of the equipment by April 14
7. Start production operations April 22

MAN-POWER REQUIREMENTS

Total = 10 additional employees

CHAPTER 19- IMPLEMENTATION

"The business model"

Understanding the *rules* is important in implementing the business plan. A superficial subjective observation is not adequate. If you based a business model and decision upon a *small sample* observation, it is likely that your business model would be inaccurate and the sale of product smaller than projected.

I have observed that the factors which have a significant major effect on the nature of conducting business is dependent upon addressing three significant rules of business conduct, these are; conducting business in an honest, ethical, legal manner. It may seem obvious that this is an encompassing *code of behavior,* it is more important than many companies realize.

"Identifying the business needs"

A most significant part of launching and sustaining a business enterprise is the financing of the business. There are many business opportunities where competition exists for limited financial resources. Enterprises engaged in fundamental research or R&D initially require venture capital or *seed money* well in advance of producing product for the market and obtaining income. Companies engaging in innovating or significant improvement products or services, often require capitalization to launch the resulting product for securing additional resources, prior to a public stock offering in the company through an IPO. Monies are required to *ramping up* production volume or expanding product lines, the need for financial strategies and plans is a *critical* role of management.

"Acquiring capital"

The acquisition of capital through bank loans and other venture capital sources requires preparation and diligence. Securing the proper resources to prepare the *plan* and present the *proposal* involves interfacing with business management personnel. Individuals responsible for accounting and financial matters will be involved in performing *due diligence* and reporting results to the responsible individuals who would provide the required financing, or who may require hiring outside sources to accomplish the task.

Venture capital firms have access to individuals or companies with training in marketing research, business administration or business management to evaluate the viability of proposed financial commitments. Capital is a commodity in short supply. Previous experience through words and deeds are ways for determining the capability of the enterprise as well as the results of the participants. It behooves a company to form a strong team of highly motivated and talented individuals to discharge the duties of managing the company, people who understand the potential of the product or service and who have the discipline and knowledge that will guide the company through the ensuing path toward success. An enterprise that *goes public* has a fiduciary responsibility to provide facts concerning the business on a periodic basis as defined by law. It also must make the workings of the company transparent to the extent possible to provide shareholders and other invested parties the information required to make an informed decision as to the holding, acquisition or sale of shares in the company.

"Stockholder-shareholder"

Many people have interests in the financial and business affairs of a company. The *stockholders* represent one part. The company's *employees*, and in some cases *suppliers* to the company, comprise a group now known as *stakeholders*. These interests are also involved with maintaining the health of the company. The future of a company involves the desire and ability of employees to invest their time and efforts in the company's behalf. Union interests are part of a company business model, in some instances, since they enter into contract, which have a direct bearing on the successful competition in the market and should reflect an appropriate factor in the plans of the business.

In situations where the enterprise is a participant in foreign ventures it is important for the company to understand the dynamics of the culture and political considerations involved with doing business in that country both from the labor and the nature of the environment under which business is conducted. Industries and services that are controlled by a government, or government agency, needs a thorough understanding of the regulatory requirements and the paths that must be traveled in successfully navigating the process toward permission to market the product or service. Product, or service marketed in foreign countries also may require compliance with sometimes complex and detail requirements uncommon to the U.S. based companies. The investment is often in time, money, personnel and resources that may be burdensome and costly beyond those anticipated.

"Outsourcing I"

It may be beneficial for the enterprise to participate in the outsourcing of part or a significant amount of the production of product or the providing of services. Outsourcing was until last century done within the U.S. utilizing contract manufacturers, suppliers of services, such as consultants, that were available to enterprises.

During the later part of the twentieth century, enterprises recognized that foreign companies have competent organizations capable of providing needed support services to worldwide and national companies. The progress in technology and education have made it economically advantages for many companies to *outsource* product or services, manufacturing operations, and obtaining fabricated and generated supplies or materials used in products. The lower labor costs coupled with the expanded high quality capability offered in this manner, has resulted in development of both national and international business and economies.

Detail analysis is required when outsourcing to foreign countries. There are tradeoffs that when fully understood may affect a decision to proceed with the activity or to change the dynamics of engagement. It is important to recognize the inherent difference in dealing with countries that have cultural norms differing from those in the U.S.

Countries in regions where the subjective aspect of business is important need to be recognized and behavior methods learned. Business conducted in the Asian sphere takes place as a *respectful* protocol. Directness is not respectful in conducting business activity in many countries. In the European sphere, engaging in social interaction is the prelude to getting down to business. The performance of business in most of the world takes place within a *gracious* and *respectful* environment. Communication depends upon the ability to understand others, both in word and meaning, against a background of culture. Americans have frequently behaved *aggressively and arrogantly*, as viewed by business people in many countries.

"Outsourcing II"

Establishment of a business relationship involves both a *contractual* agreement and an *understanding* between parties. The impact of your business needs on the *outsource* manufacturers business capacity, must be recognized in how your business will be conducted with the outsource manufacturer or service, namely what share of their business does your business represent both on a current basis as well as future growth. If you represent a significant portion of the outsource manufacturer or service business, current and future planning should consider what you may expect of their priority in delivering product in the quantity and on time that was established by contract or service agreed to be performed. However, if your order or required service is small in comparison with their existing business, delays in efficiencies in satisfying your needs or other deficiencies in performance may occur.

There are factors such as; standardization of measurement of linear dimension and volume, sampling inspection methods and analysis, verification and compliance with your requirements either *on site*, through agreed upon *third party,* and frequent assessment visits will be required. The purpose of these comments is not to discourage entering into outsourcing, but to make it clear that it is not the same *business as usual.*

The introduction of *Strategic Alliances* has expanded the availability of higher volume product and services in complementary ways to enhance the scope and depth of organizations worldwide, with the advantage of cost reduction and greater availability of product and services.

The Art of Business
"The measurements"

The objective of a business is to make a profit. The goal is to provide benefit and value to the *customer* in a cost effective manner, which is *essential* in meeting the objective. In order to achieve both the objective and the goal requires and ongoing measure of the variables which constitute the *pulse of the business.* The reporting on the status of the business requires the exercise of accounting principles and presenting the results on a periodic basis. The evaluation of the *state* of the business requires both a definition of the variables and the collection of objective data.

Three critical measures, which determine the state of the business financially, are Cost, Revenue and Profit. These terms are arrived at using rules defined by those practicing the *art* of accounting. All businesses are different regarding the specifics used to determine these factors. These measures are not governed by absolutes hence they utilize the exercise of judgment in determining results.

The Science of Business "Technology"

In today's environment, computer technology has provided a means to project happenings or scenarios, and the analysis of numbers under varying conditions. This is helpful in another way. It permits utilizing mathematical/scientific modeling. It also provides a basis for extrapolating results and for projecting the likelihood of meeting endpoints. This provides an early warning or proof of feasibility and enhances the running of the business.

The business *planning* function is one example where mathematical modeling is used. Management of Research and Development programs require tracking to determine compliance with requirements. Project Managers, assign individuals to control the elements of the program and their performance tracked and expenses identified.

In product technology business, as well as service industries, computers have extended the capability for conducting business matters. Not only for generating *documents*, but for generating and tracking data on *spreadsheets* for control of purchasing inventory and production, *databases* for providing a common source of information, providing project definition and *tracking* of progress toward completion within established timelines, endpoints, and defined milestones. *Presentations* graphics, photos, and audio-visual information are prepared and displayed to the numerous participants at meetings, conferences, and communicated to specific individuals.

The implementation of scientific principles is a method for identification of risk, analysis of data, and proof of technology. Conducting business by implementation of programs and projects is critical to success.

Observation: Art and Science of Business

A review of recorded history, and pre historical artifacts, has illustrated characteristics of 'humans', which have enabled us to reach this point in time.

Some of the characteristics provide a portal through which successful evolutionary influences have traveled by our genetic print. Other factors have had profound influence, such as actions that confer a survival benefit and still others which are a result of development and learning. In this somewhat complex soup of conditions, the arts and sciences have developed an attempt to permit a better understanding of ourselves, and the world around us.

Curiosity is an inherent trait that has a profound effect on the development of our lineage. Curiosity and reason are inherent 'human' factors exhibited at a very early age. Infants reach out toward sounds, sights, and smell to identify and learn about objects, feelings, and interaction with the environment. This develops into a curiosity about 'how things work', and the typical question of the young child "Why is the sky blue", and the desire to decode the mystery around us.

Our curiosity drives us to seek answers to questions concerning purpose, methods, acts, though reasoned thinking, proof of principle, experimentation as trial and error, and communication between people to benefit from the discovery and knowledge of others.

The road traveled has resulted in the discoveries of the 'laws' of science, the refinement of practices, and the development of means which benefit mankind. It has also resulted in huge damage, the perfection of the means of human destruction for one. Even when one accounts for the minuses, on balance the direction has been in a continual positive direction.

This curiosity has been responsible for the development of the 'arts and sciences'.

The discipline required in science, of absolute proof of validity, has provided us with a 'bed rock' such that expansion of concepts and ideas add, to a fundamentally sound foundation.

The arts however, are an evolving landscape that provides the mechanism for growth and development and expansion into areas previously unexplored. It has made it possible for the 'artist' to express their unique talent to create and accomplish.

A combination of these two aspects of human development occurs in the practice of the medical profession. The medical 'scientist' can develop the 'tools' for diagnosis, treatment and mitigation of many disease states, it is the surgeon who has developed the means for translating the technology into the practice of curative and mitigating procedures in the operating room. This is an example of how medical art and medical science act together to accomplish a result that is greater than the sum of the parts.

There are a number of subjects identified incorrectly, as sciences. These include 'political science' and 'governmental science'. In order to define business as a science there would need to be rigorous demonstration in establishing 'truth' and a 100% certainty in the results of the scientific 'proof of theory'. Not 80% of the time, not 90% of the time, not even 99.5% of the time, but only 100% true.

There are other life activities where the mantel of 'truth' is assigned, in a court of law, the purpose of the adversarial process is to present each lawyers 'version' of the' facts' in order to reach the 'truth'. In reality, this arrival at 'truth' is often done mainly though superior professional skills rather than proof. The judge charges a jury thus; "it is up to you the jurors to determine the facts in this matter". In the civil justice system there is a need for the jury to reach a verdict based upon a 'preponderance of evidence' in a civil case, and proof beyond a 'reasonable doubt' in a criminal case. In both of these conditions there is infrequent determination based upon the certainty of the 'scientific method' at arriving at the 'facts'. It is not science.

This is not to dismiss out of hand the 'state of the art' practiced in various areas of life. What is necessary is to understand the limitations that exist in human endeavor and strive to improve upon our knowledge and practices.

In presenting 'small business and human growth and development' metaphorically, the aim is to illustrate the comparable phases of development through which each path passes, in the process of development. So far, human development is an ongoing 'scientific process', and the development of business is still an 'art'. We may learn from human development, how to improve our viability, as it relates to a business.

The intent of this book is to provide insights into relationships between science and empirical experiences. This book is the first in a series of books intended to provide insight into the path of life's adventure.

Methods for Conducting Business
"Rules and methods"

Business takes place within a backdrop of previous history, current reality, and anticipated discovery. In this context, a business or service needs to be aware of the conventions of business dealings that apply to the emerging enterprise. In dealing in an existing environment, change can be either an advantage, or disadvantage. Often, change is an *unknown* and feared, and for others it may be an opportunity for improvement or accomplishment. Hence, in introducing new product it is important to size up the atmosphere where the product will fit within the needs of the market, and determine the potential of the product or service within the anticipated bounds of convention or acceptance. It may require preparation and incorporation of user-friendly *ergonomics*, targeted preference, or creation of a new market segment.

The rules of the game relates to the type of business, and the channels for sale and communication.

For introducing new product, or service, numerous potential *methods* exist that need to be explored. For the introduction of an improved version of an existing product or service, or a different product or service, a unique strategy may be required. The strategy may focus only on sale into an existing market, where the objective is to gain market share, or may be a comprehensive marketing effort for developing a market for the new product. Representatives of the enterprise need to address the client/customer/user/ patient needs in a professional manner consistent with the organizations philosophy, principles and policy.

Engaging the Marketplace
"The marketplace, is where it counts"

The marketplace is where goods, services, and ideas, are exchanged for; money, bartered goods, or services. The market left unfettered or unconstrained by restrictive legal mandates, is free to exchange between parties based upon the perceived value for the goods or services offered [2]. In its actions, the marketplace is the measure of value determined only by buyer and seller. It does not always act on a *one-on-one* basis, since third parties may enter into the process. When a third party is between buyer and seller, the party becomes the seller (or buyer) with the process repeated through the actions of the new seller (or buyer). For example, companies often sell product through distributors who stock and sell the company's product directly to the end user, or in some cases through sales personnel, hence the company has engaged an *agent* in the transaction. In fact, the company maintains liability for the performance of the product or service.

When service is done by a professional, or with a third party, the performance still rests with the initial service provider, such as with the case of a physician and surgeon who engages another physician in treating the patient.

Both the public and the politician often ask the question regarding *oversight* of an enterprise. The role that government often has taken is that of *enforcer*, whereas business ventures see their role as an *ethical* dispenser of goods and services. The public is the ultimate customer/user of the product/service. Unfettered competition acts as the means for achieving a fair and consistent market for products and ideas. Selling or offering goods and service to the marketplace requires an understanding of the *turf*. The role that an enterprise takes requires analysis of a number of factors. These factors involve potential sales or service volume, the pricing, and profit anticipated. It is important to recognize that the market is *fluid*. It is not static, so when choosing the dynamics that may apply to both now and future expectations, that must be considered. The question becomes a calculation of risk/benefit ratio for providing the product or service. This is especially true for business based upon technologic significance. In the space of a decade, what was a *sure thing* may be outdated in 3, 5, 7, or 10 years. A venture that seeks to compete in an established market needs to understand the *state-of-the art* that applies to the product, or service, and to obtain reasoned and detail input from valid sources to assess the true potential. Market research firms make their mark on the business picture by conducting research projects to assess the potential in the wide range of products and services. In local, national, and international business, it is necessary to understand the environment in order to provide significant and accurate projections of future need.

A further question arises regarding the nature of the enterprise objectives. Three factors are important to consider when a company is planning to introduce a new concept product. ; 1) time that it will likely take to complete the process from design, development and manufacturing of the product to introduction into the market, 2) the cost of developing and producing the product, 3) the potential for payback on the investment (Return On Investment) and the time that it will take to reach the desired level in the marketplace. Additionally, questions concerning product *life expectancy* in the market and the competitive landscape for exclusivity are factors requiring analysis. If a company is planning on introducing a better *me too product* the questions that need to be answered is similar to that required for a new concept product, as well as determining market share that is expected for this product against the established competitors.

Conducting Business in a Regulated Environment "Learning to deal with regulations"

Business on a *one to one* basis was, in the past, the method used to conduct business. This was the way that people transacted all forms of exchange. Transaction based upon *mutual trust* developed from years of experience. Hence, there was no thought of outside intervention in the transaction. Starting in the 20th century, *government intervention* in all business resulted in *government regulation*. All business today takes place within a *regulated* environment. It is a matter *of to what extent it occurs*, it is not a question of if *regulation is imposed* instead it is a question of *how much* is applicable. The imposition of regulation has had a direct impact of the *freedom* in the market place and has likely curtailed innovation of product. [2]

To practice a service, to manufacture and sell a product, to conduct sale of a commodity, to trade stock, perform a banking function, to farm and sell produce, and conduct *any* other business all require obtaining permission from *government agencies*, either/or Federal, State, Local or International Bodies.

This may require obtaining permits, registration for permission to collect sales/local taxes, planning and zoning permission, Environmental Impact Reporting approval from all environment bodies as well as for the use of water, for the disposal of waste/pollution, for rights to connect to utilities, etc. Additionally, if your trade is between states, the permit and approval process may involve agencies such as; EPA, OSHA, FDA, ICC, FTC, IRS, and other *alphabet* Federal Government agencies.

Business today has expanded into areas beyond previous imagination. During the early twentieth century innovation and discovery led to development and marketing of items that have a direct effect, on the risk to and safety of the user as well as those who may be affected by their actions.

Prior to that time, the only safety concerns were associated with direct injury or sickness. If a horse ran over a person, a building feel down, a person was shot, or forces of nature affected their path they were either injured or they died. If a person(s) was afflicted with a disease, the patient recovered, or they died. The lifestyle and events affecting people's survival was unsophisticated. Unknown risks to health and safety affected a person's life.

During the third decade of the twentieth century, there was an awareness of the expansion of available items and products that were capable of enhancing life, as well as extending life, however, this created risks that required understanding and mitigation. Prior to discovery of the uses for electricity, installation of railroads, production of automobiles, food packaging and handling and transportation, there was little need to address the risk that accompanied use of these innovations. People were injured or died of errors and faults with products from this new technology.

In recognition of the events that were occurring, the federal government enacted laws that established agencies to improve health and safety issues affecting the public. For example, the congress established the Food and Drug Administration, under the Food, Drug and Cosmetic Act.

Managing Change
"Life: learning to deal with change"

During the growth and development of a business/ enterprise change in management and organization will likely occur. One day a senior member of the company management will call a meeting, or send a memo or e-mail announcing that a change has taken place. The change involves the departure/reassignment of an individual or department. Many reasons are stated. For example, to pursue another business opportunity (read; they resigned, or was fired), to retire, to move to another role in the company (read; they likely did not get the job done). When a person unfortunately died, *a new position* opened up (read; they need to find a place for someone related to the President or family), or the expansion of a business function. The cause may be stated as due to an increases in sales, development of a new/changed product or product line, realigning the structure to reduce cost (outsourcing). The impact of the *change* can be minor, in the case of a readjustment in responsibilities, or will likely be severe as in the case of new senior management realignment and hiring. The effect upon the company personnel, their working *family*, can be as major as an event in the employee's actual family.

The changes may result in an atmosphere of formality that may have previously been low-key management and easy exchange of communication with management.

The change may create a different environment where there is a more formal structured organization and where communication between the individual and the organizations management requires formality and scheduling. There also may be a change in the structure of the responsibilities and authorities of the individual. The individual may have had responsibility for the results of their efforts and having the authority to take decisions.

The new environment may result in organized participation as a member of a *team* where there is a *shared* and *group accountability* structure. The result may be significant change in efficiencies, work environment and individual satisfaction which could cause a *shake up* and people leaving for *greener pastures* to a company that better suites their individual working needs and where they receive recognition for their individual accomplishments. This analysis is valid for any enterprise where more than a few people are involved in the performance of the company/business. In offices, for example, the office staff typically reports to an office manager, in a professional enterprise such as medical, accounting, engineering, etc. there is usually an individual who is directly involved with both the boss and the team and coordinates and manages the operational activities.

The one *constant* in life is *change*. The universe and its contents are in a state of flux, so why do some people look upon change as an aberrant event? Newton's Law of Inertia states that things at rest tend to stay at rest, whereas things in motion tend to stay in motion, hence it takes effort/energy to go from a resting state to one of motion and vice-versa. Emotionally, change, is considered a waste of effort and avoided.

Anecdote: Defining Responsibility
in an Organization

It was clear that the assignment of responsibility and roles at a company that had encountered difficulties in completing tasks in a timely basis was due to management issues. The difficulty centered in how the office staff would process customer orders, purchase materials, and interfacing with the customers. Observing the work practices and the interface between the owner and the office personnel revealed the cause of the problem.

In an interview with the office employees, on a one by one basis, revealed that each person had a different idea as to what each of their responsibilities were and to whom they reported. They stated that various managers continually preempted the work assignments given to them by other managers.

It was clear that the office lacked organization and well defined responsibilities and supervision.

There was a concept of crisis management often found in small companies, particularly during the early growth of the company. It is extremely important that this not go on for long. It is a source of dissatisfaction, frustration, and inefficiency.

"Dealing with meaningful change"

Having stated a tendency for avoiding change let us look at how *change* may be both necessary and rewarding. Change for the *sake of change*, does not provide value added. Too many times the need for *change* is a reason for asserting *relevance*, rather than for a purpose of increasing efficiency, improvement in profitability, increase in value, improving employment position, or the market, or improvement in providing service. Demonstration for the need for change has value when it is a factual need. Outlining the rationale toward achieving a defined result and the endpoint, estimation of the benefit/risk ratio including return on investment, the cost and the resources required is an analysis needed to achieve beneficial results.

A plan for accomplishing the change, selling the change process to those affected by the change, recognizing that change affects both perception and reality, is recognition that people respond differently to change based upon their previous experiences in life. It is important to define both the need for change and to structure the change process in order to present a rational and compelling reason.

A philosophic change has occurred in the management of resources, namely people, in recent years. Archaic business management methods have evolved into a new *paradigm*.

The new paradigm considers all participants in the company activities as being *stakeholders*. Those who exercise these roles are encouraged to participate, by changing from their more *classical* roles of employees/workers, suppliers/material providers, buyers/users, to that of participants in the business.

Anecdote: A New position and others concern

The company, a Medical Device company, had three facilities on the West Coast. The Operations head of one of these facilities had left the company, and another Senior Director was chosen to operate the facility.

During the transition, the Vice President of Operations met at the facility to hold a series of meetings with employees in each of the functional departments. After each meeting, a Q and A session took place to elicit comments and suggestions.

The first of the meetings was with the Engineering Department personnel. The engineering employees asked about plans and matters concerning the development of new products and changes to improve products.

The next meeting was with the Production Test Technicians whose questions concerned obtaining new test equipment and if we were going to change shifts and hours.

The last meeting was with the Production Operators whose questions were quite different. One person asked the question, "If a worker was late, what would the company do regarding docking her pay". Another was concerned about what the company would do about people telling gossip about someone if it was not true. Their question was would the person telling these lies be punished.

This illustrates that people have different concerns and interests about the matters that they perceive has an effect upon them, their future, their security, and the relationships with other employees and management.

"Adopting new methods"

This new *paradigm* defines *roles* in a new way. It establishes a new *activism* amongst players in the game. Management personnel exercising their responsibility and authority, as defined by the principals in the company, made *decisions* previously. The *Organization* defined these responsibilities, authorities and accountabilities of the management members.

During the expansion of the Defense Industry in the 1950's and beyond, contracting firms in concert with the applicable Government Agencies, introduced a new project and program management *scheme*. The methods provided visibility by conducting *committee meetings* and generating reports. This led to endless meetings to discuss progress, issues, reviews, action plans. A famous saying resulted from this methodology, "A zebra is a horse designed by a committee". In the environment where *money* was not a significant issue, which was the case then, expenditures of resources were second to meeting the end point as close to schedule as possible. Changes have evolved from those *primitive* methods, to a new *doctrine* of modern management of business.

This current trend is toward *management* by *committee*, where *teams* provide the *input* and *decision* making in many areas of the company operations. The teams are set up with a *facilitator* who guides the efforts based upon the collective inputs of the team members, using as a guide the proposed need defined by management. The team assigns and defines goals and objectives. Discussion of progress toward achieving the goals and objectives, take place in *meetings*. Changes in carrying out the assignments are dependent on the team's perceived or defined duties.

A primary difficulty that this has had in instituting team methods is that of *shared* management and accountability where no *individual,* is responsible or accountable for achieving, or failure to achieve the results planned. The team method tends to subordinate individuality, as witness by the expression there is no "I" in team!

Anecdote: Just in Time and other methods

"The latest is not always the greatest!"

Since the early 1950s, there has been a continuing effort to accelerate the improvement of business. This has resulted in the formulation and experimentation with a number of concepts. Books such as "In search of Excellence" was published and was based upon the writers analysis of a number of big companies and how their experiences in changing the way that they were doing business had a significant effect on their productivity and profitability. A stream of books outlining other methods, such as the "Team of Teams", and "The One Minute Manager", etc followed.

The next comments are not a critique of new management techniques and methods they are to point out the need to understand the basis of the claims and the specificity of the applicability of new systems and methods to any specific business.

It is valuable that books and curricula are available to help teach the value and significance of evolving business methods. Many of these found their way into business courses at Universities, and in MBA projects.

As an example of a popular method was the 'just in time' concept developed for manufacturing in Japan. This method, described as an innovation worthy of emulating in US businesses.

This concept developed by an Industrial Engineer named Shigeo Shingo, a degreed Japanese engineer and President of the Institute of Management Improvement in Tokyo Japan. Mr. Shingo introduced this and other concepts starting in 1946 at Hitachi, Ltd, which continued with employee training of his methods at Toyota in 1970 [4] During his experience in the Japanese Railroad system Mr. Shingo developed the 'Just In Time' (JIT) concept during the 1930's. The method took advantage of characteristics of the Japanese working ethic and culture. Namely, working for a "Company" is a commitment and a loyalty above all other considerations. Production of product is under a structured system and performed in a disciplined manner. Another factor is the structure of business in Japan. In Japan, there are only a few major conglomerate companies, where each company manufactures a very wide range of products. For example, one conglomerate manufactures automobiles, HI Def televisions, Printers, Computers, DVDs, pharmaceuticals, and other consumer products. The other major factor is that each of these companies 'own' the company that 'supplies' parts and materials to that company, hence when materials and parts are needed the supplier produces the required product at the required rate at the required time. Hence, JIT is a natural evolution in the supply chain.

The difficulty in transferring this concept from a Japanese company environment to a US company is both a cultural and functional inequality. In the US, each company is in completion with other companies for the output of suppliers, hence are typically not in a position to make 'demands' for priority deliveries and sole attention, unless the producer is a major source of the supplier's business whereby he may impose unusual or demanding requirements. A GE or GM or Motorola may receive preferential service however, most medium and small size companies are just going to have to negotiate the best fit for their needs.

Inside the manufacturer's factory, the differences in work ethics, habits, culture, dedication is again a difference between Japan and the US companies. In the US, working people are 'individuals' and work for a living. Although they may look upon the company in a positive light and recognize the benefits to self as well as family, it does not mean that the worker in the US is looking at a commitment for their entire working life.

> *There have been a number of books published with the objective of providing a 'better' way to utilize human resources. The following examples demonstrate this approach.*
>
> *Six Sigma, Lean Production, Team of Teams, Quality Circles, and others methods, have been developed for industry and other work environments with the goal of improvement of efficiency and productivity. Although many good ideas have been developed and implemented, the 'success rate' has rarely met the advertised claims.*

Stakeholders are in a sense the *new* unions, in that they monitor business practices, business sales, business ethics, business compensation, etc. The *stakeholders* are concerned with such matters as hiring rates, layoffs, discipline, profitability, and strive to make sure that everyone gets their *fair share.*

"The test"

The *stakeholder,* who may *also* be a *stockholder,* is now a partner with the *stockholder* in decision-making and the conduct of many businesses. The emphasis is that the stakeholder has as much of an investment interest in the company as the shareholder, since the stakeholder success is dependent upon how management directs the company, hence their role is one of *activism* in making sure that company management is responsive to their needs. The stockholders put their money into the company via stock or bonds. They do this *at risk* having determined that the risk is sound based upon the history and projected future of the company. When the company achieves its anticipated goals, it may result in the sharing of profits as reflected in the quarterly earnings statements or stock value growth, other times the company may fall short of expectations. However, the stockholder votes with their money. An employee is also free as an individual to exercise their judgment by staying employed at the company or looking for another job.

If the company is not meeting expectations or promises, the results are visible and the employee may elect to exercise their displeasure by selling the stock and/or leaving the company. The judgment is swift and decisive and clearly transmits this verdict to management.

The Technology-Enterprise Revolution
"History of the new technology"

In past times, the marketing and *sale* of a product, commodity or a service took place based upon a competition with others engaged in the same or similar activity. The sale of commodities and harvested food products took place at the local emporium/merchant. In locations where people lived and worked in cities, people would purchase food from butchers, bakers, green grocers, fish stores. Health and other professional and trade services were available from the local Doctor, Lawyer, Barber, Plumber, etc.

The birth of industrialization created a major shift in that *paradigm*. With the advent of inventive technology and creativity in design and development of both product and services, new products were available in the marketplace. This shift brought about a philosophic development that is the major driving force of business since then to today. The axiom was and is *if you can make it, you can sell it*. It became clear that a new source of creating wealth is through *innovation,* where "Invention is the conversion of cash into ideas. Innovation is the conversion of ideas into cash." [5)]

The period between 1850 and 2000 was 150 years of *explosion* in invention and application and with it a range of progress previously unknown during the history of man. The Alexander Graham Bell's, Thomas Edison's, Henry Ford's, Bill Gates', Jonas Salk's, Enrique Fermi (and all like them), were and are the driving force. It is only when inventions and innovation occurs that it is possible to *sell* it.

That does not ignore the role of sales and marketing, but puts into perspective the areas where both current and future business enterprise will have the most effect.

Prior to World War II the methods of *mass production* of product was in its infancy, Henry Ford having been the pioneer. When requirements for war related product increased during the early 1940's, the methods of production were inefficient and costly. This model changed drastically as the *need* for producing vast numbers of items in a very short time caused a major change in techniques and methods deployed by industry. This was truly the beginning of what was the *Technology-Enterprise Revolution*. One of the major issues that surfaced was the poor reliability of equipment. Prior to the 1940's, there was little consideration given to moving-shipping-transportation of military equipment around the world and assuring that the equipment functioned correctly upon receipt and setup. A review of the history of that time reveals that the issues were due to the methods of design and development of reliable, durable and environmental robust product that was imperative for the *war* effort.

The first major change was the development of requirements for environmental testing of products to determine and demonstrate the suitability of the equipment such as that of tanks, aircraft, automobiles, guns, radios, etc. that had to operate in desserts, in snow and rain, on oceans, at high altitudes, or rough terrain. Government contracts defined and incorporated requirements for tests and specified methods. These contracts were awarded to manufacturers and engineering companies. The result of this effort was a significant reduction in *out of box rate of failure* (Figure D).

A major change made the conduct of business different. Automobiles were mass-produced starting in the 1920's only a little less than two decades before the War effort. The method of manufacturing consisted of the *funnel* approach to product manufacturing. In which, parts were feed into the beginning of the process and then rejects were *filtered out* as the product moved through the line until some number of *good* product made it through the entire production line the first time through. Then reworking of rejected product took place to make it *good* so it would pass.

The introduction of *quality control techniques* changed the business philosophy and the methods for conducting business. Government contracts mandated quality control as a part of the requirements. *Quality Inspection* criteria became a specific requirement. Industry came to realize that in order to meet with the inspection requirements they needed to make an investment in both the techniques tools/methods and the structure of the manufacturing operation, which took place from the 1940's on. Mass production of reliable and durable products became the *norm* and business recognized the benefit of increase in efficiency and reduction of cost to produce product. The manufacture of a reliable product required determining the soundness of the product design using a structured testing program to assure that the design was *capable* of achieving a highly reliable product. Requirements for components and parts used in manufacturing the product had to meet specifically defined criteria established during the design stages. The *Quality Inspection* function inspected the components and parts used in products to determine compliance with the *specified requirements*. Acceptable parts that met specifications went on to manufacturing, at the *beginning* of the manufacturing process. The objective was for the manufacturing processes to maintain the inherent reliability of the components and the product as it went through the production process hence resulting in a higher yield of good product.

Three Nobel Prize winning scientists invented a semiconductor device, later known as the "Transistor", in 1947. The Bell Telephone Systems, Bell Laboratories, a part of the American Telephone and Telegraph Company (AT&T) employed the three inventors. The *transistor* opened up an entirely new realm of innovation. It made possible the mass production and commercialization of hitherto before expensive and limited technology products of that era. The transistor and its further development into Integrated Circuits (IC's) and Microprocessors made it possible to perform an overwhelming number of complex tasks easily and fast. The development of the Computer and Internet as well as the iPod, HDTV, and Microwaves etc., are a result of the expansion of this technology. The design development and manufacture of large volume low cost efficient components and products that are both *reliable* and inexpensive continues to fuel the technology/ business revolution.

The Art and Science of Problem Solving

Problems that arise in or with business enterprises are common. How problems occur and how they are mitigated is dependent upon numerous factors which are contingent upon the nature and severity of the problem.

Successful problem solving is predicated upon the method used to identify, investigate, analyze, evaluate, determining the root causes of the problem, instituting corrective/preventive action, and evaluating the effectiveness of the corrective/preventive action taken toward preventing recurrence.

There are two approaches that are significant in this process; an *artful* approach, a *scientific* approach. The artful approach looks upon a problem as a subjective assessment of a matter of form, substance, and seek solution by finesse. A trial and error approach to resolving the problem in the first, second, or third, etc. attempt is one method toward problem solving. On the other hand, a scientific approach is an objective assessment of all the factors involved in the problem and a systematic analysis and defined methods for determining the basis of the problem by investigation, evaluation and corrective action, followed by tracking results to determine if the action resolved the problem from recurring. The range of problems in a business or service enterprise typically is extensive. The ability to apply resources in a formal and defined systematic manner to achieve results and resolution requires an understanding of the significance of the problem. The significance of a problem is specific to the impact upon the business, health or safety if it is a high risk or major hazard; hence not all problems are equal and do not require the same focus and application of scarce resources.

Anecdote: Quid pro Quo exchange between people

Quid pro Quo can be a free exchange of property, or an act of stealing if done under fraud or by plunder.

When individuals engage in free, unforced, exchange of the results of their labor or property for another form of 'equal' value, both parties in the transaction consider the results equitable. The nature of 'Business' is predicated upon this fact. Verbal or written contracts between individuals, between business, and between each other, are best when based upon Quid pro Quo criteria.

In dealing and interacting with people, it is relevant to ascertain the basis of any exchange. The key is value given for value received.

A now retired colleague was a successful program manager, and always carried around his 'toolbox' in 'dealing' with people and problems.

His 'toolbox' did not contain pliers, wrenches, saws, hammers, or other physical tools. He used the items in his toolbox to exchange that which he needed for that which the other party wanted. As an example: A newly developed product was being 'transferred' from R&D to Product Manufacturing. The product contained a critical part manufactured by a supplier. The component used in the medical device, an innovation of tremendous potential in improving sick people's health, was late in delivery due to technical issues. . A key to getting the product to market on time was in expediting the manufacture of the critical component.

An extraordinary effort was required from the supplier's personnel to expedite the manufacturing. The period between Christmas and New Years was a Holiday vacation time and no one scheduled or inclined to work during this period. However, we needed the parts and time was critical toward achieving the marketing window planned.

The program manger was committed to accommodate our schedule and looked in his "toolbox" for the tools to do the 'job'. He approached the Production Manager, who he knew well, with the proposition that he would exchange a two days paid holiday for each day worked by anyone in his department if the schedule was met, including him. The Production Manger said that he did not know if the employees would be willing to exchange some of their holiday time for two days pay. The program manager asked if he could ask them individually. He approached them with the proposition. The Program Manager 'sweetened the pot' by making an offer to them allowing them to bring any two guests to a trip to Disneyland in compensation for their cooperation. Almost all of the employees agreed. The exchange, Quid pro Quo, resulted not only in meeting the schedule, but also cemented the relationship with the customer, who proceeded to sell the product and to significantly increase the order of parts from the supplier. It truly was a win-win situation!

Having noticed that 'successful problem solvers' may be of different stripes, they all have a basic characteristic in common. These are; the ability to define the problem thoroughly, capable of performing a logical and analytical investigation, ability to effectively utilize resources, an undeterred effort to obtain a solution to the problem, a systematic approach, and the confidence that the problem can and will be solved.

Allen M.Hans, Ph.D.

The Methods Used For Problem Solving

Most problems associated with technology and health care related businesses require a systematic and thorough analysis since the impact upon the customer/user/client/patient may be critical to their health, welfare, or ability to function in a safe manner. Problems associated with health or safety concerns arise in three areas; design and development of the product, manufacturing and delivery of the product, communicating proper use of the items sold.

In the first part of the last century simplicity of product design and manufacturing resulted in highly visible problems when they occurred; the item broke, shattered, resulted in causing fire, caused flooding, resulted in death or serious injury, etc. During the later part of the twentieth century, the number of and significance of problem occurrence increased greatly and in many cases did not show up in a manner that indicated there was a problem until it had migrated to a major issue or resulted in catastrophic effects and proportions.

With the advent of high-speed transportation, nuclear energy, biological products, health care diagnostic/curative equipment, equipment for monitoring and analyzing disease and health problems made the discovery and mitigation of problems more critical to the health and safety of the public. Hence, the pursuit of scientific methods to identify, correct and prevent problems from affecting multitudes of people all over the world occurred. Not only time or quantity, but also significance and extent of potential for causing actual injury or damage needs to considered. In this regard, our language has been changed to include new meaning for these events, which include; *recalls, warnings, cautions, contraindications and hazardous,* dangerous to name a few examples. These terms along with instant communications makes the significance of timely identification and mitigation critical.

Anecdote: Examples of Problem Solving

Problem solving involving people

Case A:

A problem involved work punctuality of an employee.

Having previous little experience in dealing with this type of problem help was requested from the company Vice-President. The VP was an 'older gentleman', who had been in management positions for many years. A meeting was set up in his office to discuss this dilemma. His office was quite Spartan. His office consisted of one bookcase a metal desk, two chairs, one behind the desk and one in front of his desk. His in box and out box were empty.

He was reading the Wall Street journal upon arrival at his office. Upon entering his office, he asked about the health and welfare of the family.

He then asked what the problem was that needed discussion. We discussed the issue and the circumstances concerning this employee's chronic lateness to work even though his performance was very good.

He then asked how the problem was so far, being handled. The response was that there was a meeting with the employee on several occasions and we discussed his tardiness with him.

When the description of the problem was through, he simply asked, "What do you think you should do about the situation". A number of paths and choices were identified which were meaningful. He then asked "Which path and choices do you think are appropriate" and which would be the best choice. I made a decision and discussed the implementation with him. He then said that it "made sense" to him, and I thanked him and left his office.

On the way back to my office, it became apparent that 'I' had come up with a solution to the problem. Wow, how smart 'my boss' was!

Case B:

As Operation Manager at a Mexican company owned by a US owner, we encountered frequent personnel problems that required resolution.

During one visit to Mexico, a Senior Manager came into the office and asked if we could talk. She sat down and said that things were not going well. She said that another Senior Manager was trying to 'sabotage' her work and 'usurp her authority'. She went on to say this manager was 'bossy' and 'aggressive'. She then asked me to" immediately take action with her (the other manager) and make her stop her behavior."

The meeting concluded with the statement further discussion would take place when the results of the evaluation were determined.

The other manager was asked to come into the office, and asked how things were going. She said that the 'other' manager had been 'hostile' toward her regarding a job that she 'routinely' performs, which she has responsibility for, for some time. She further stated that the other manager was acting 'mean' and 'undermined' her position.

Two things were involved, 1) both managers were highly active and assertive people, and 2) they were both *excellent workers who had been part of the success of the company. In the past these particular women had 'locked horns', and that neither would 'budge' if they felt threatened or demeaned.*

This posed an interesting but potentially damaging issue to the company.

I realized that this would not be resolved by either 'taking sides', or by disciplining one or both participants, hence the issue would need to be resolved by recognition of the actual issue, and focusing on the benefit of resolving the problem, to both parties.

I called both of them to my office and after they had sat down I stated that both of them are valuable employees to the company and that I have no intention of 'taking sides' and went on to say that I wanted to hear both sides of the issue from each of them, and then proceed from there. They each stated that they wanted to get along with the other, but that the intrusion into each other's area of responsibility was causing frustration and irritation.

Each of them was asked what they believed was their primary areas of responsibility. There were two areas out of the combined 8-10 areas of responsibility where there was contention.

They were then asked to describe how they would resolve these responsibility issues, they both made suggestions. It was explained to them that the fact that they were Managers and that they were both capable, they were expected to deal with each other in a Professional manner, and that they needed to hold each other's efforts in respect.

With the issue clarified, it was possible for them to see the problem and discuss solutions that were mutually accepted. "They had solved the problem".

The Competition

The changes that occurred in Science and Technology in the 20th century resulted in a 'global' effect. In the past, the Western countries were the places where invention, and innovations in design and production of product, took place.

During the late 1940's after the War, Japan, Germany and other affected countries began re-developing their industrial base and incorporating the proven methods that resulted from United States industrial growth. The United States played a major role in these efforts.

Since the 1950's countries other than the United States and Western Europe developed their own capability to manufacture highly technical products at less cost that those manufactured in the U.S. hence, *outsourcing* of components, then sub-assembly production, then products took place.

Additionally, those countries in Asia were able to utilize a highly competent work force that produced reliable product at lower wages to compete with the United States in their own production of products such as; Televisions, Radios, VCR's, Computers, etc. Today, many U.S. companies are 'partners' with foreign-based companies, and have operations in these other countries.

Additionally, the outsourcing of manufacturing has resulted in a change in the *conduct* of business. The change is not without difficulties however, the expansion into foreign markets has been a significant benefit to all parties.

This has freed up the use of *resources* previously engaged in the manufacture of product in a less efficient utilization of the capabilities of people, for use in industries and operations having a greater effect upon our economy. This is not without penalty. The cost of re-training through education and vocational schooling has not kept pace with these major dislocations of the labor pool. In a recession the impact of these 'lost jobs' is significant.

The future economy has shifted from low skill, quantity effort, to high skill service oriented labor requirements. The United States economy will benefit and potentially maintain its excellence by applying the emphasis to innovative *value added business*, as techno-centered innovation requires, for example as in the biotechnology, nanoparticle, and health related industries and services.

Investment in *people* as a *resource* has to be the focus of the future. The ability to manufacture product can be a major achievement only when the benefit of doing it in the United States and selling it internally and internationally is greater than from purchasing the item from other countries in the world. The multinational economic paradigm that exists now, and in the future, requires a renewed commitment to entrepreneurial adventure.

Anecdote: Competition Cost vs. Price

Competing in the market place requires a thorough understanding about the clients, customers or end users needs and perspective in their purchase and your sale of your product.

This became clear soon after assuming responsibility for the operation of a medical device organization. In reviewing our cost of production with the management team, and questioning the price that our items were selling for in the market.

We were competing with three other producers of the product and that it was a matter of 1-2 cents per unit that made the difference as to which company was able to sell to major distributors.

At first, it was not clear as to how this 0.5-1.0% difference between suppliers would be significant. The 'end user' of the product utilized the product in a procedure that cost the patient over $1,000!

It turned out to be a matter of volume and incremental profit' that was involved. It was not the cost of the individual product, however when volume was considered, it was the total incremental profit that was involved. It was not the cost to the medial professional, but the cost to the distributor. The sales volume that was involved was 2-3Million units per year! At that rate of sales-volume, $.02 difference/ unit actually meant a difference in $60,000 per year a very significant difference.

The Customer

Wikipedia describes "Customer", as follows:

"A customer, also *client, buyer* or *purchaser* is the buyer or user of the *paid products* of an *individual or organization*, mostly called the *supplier or seller.* This is typically through *purchasing or renting goods or services."*

Today, it is difficult to describe a *typical* customer, since there is more needed to understand how the *supply chain* functions for a specific product, service. A large difference exists between a product, a commodity, a service and the process that takes place between the product/customer interfaces. Hence, when establishing a venture in these fields, it is necessary to define these relationships early in the formative stage. An invalid estimation of this seemingly simple distinction may lead to a *less than satisfactory*, result or a *disaster*.

"The past"

In the United States, food purchasers/customers used to buy food products from a local neighborhood *'mom and pop'* shop where the proprietor knew the customer by name, and food purchasing habits.

There were different shops that sold dairy products, baked goods, fruits and vegetables needs, and other mom and pop shops that provided product for their meat and fish needs. The shops proprietors would purchase directly from the food providers, such as in fishmongers and farmers, or from centralized suppliers, dependent on location and availability. This method followed a pattern that goes back to the early days of selling and barter.

During the twentieth century, this means of purchase changed, with the advent of the Super Market. The supermarket is a one stop fits all food supplier therefore the food supplier is a businessperson who rarely has direct contact with each customer, although his representatives (clerks, stockers, managers, etc.) interface with the customer.

"Present I"

Similar changes in selling and buying methods had developed for a wide range of product and services during the past century. Product and service is available to groups and through them to individuals. Items are routinely generated and available from foreign sources and international corporations. There no longer are seasonal limitation on the availability of fresh fruits and vegetables or fish and seafood, nor are products solely in the domain of specialists. The same is true for most commodities and durables. The range of products and services available today are *worldwide* and provides an ample supply to fill the demand. Service is available through worldwide sources. Information exchange and availability makes it possible to route telephone inquiries to technicians and experts 24/7, and by optimally utilizing labor as availability when needed regardless of the different world time zones.

A business venture must identify the nature of the *supply chain* for the product or service provided in order to place the emphasis on the relationship between the various differences, as product or service is available. A particular example is in the changes in buying methods that occurred during the past century.

The manufacturer of products, have marketed their products by brand name, hence the product was *labeled* with the designated *logo* and using the product producers name. With the development of *private labeling* this situation has changed. Today many products use the sellers name on the product, manufactured by the *xyz* company located in *a b c* country and sold through a distributor *123* to the seller, using the sellers name on the product. The only restriction in selling in the United States is that the product must state the country of origin, that is, the country where the last *significant transformation of the product* occurred.

"Present II"

In many industries, the supply chain has developed in a different way. In the past individual Hospitals had purchased supplies, equipment and devices *directly* from manufacturers, sales organizations, or representatives or distributors. Today, hospital *chains*, or hospital *cooperatives* are purchasing needed items by combining into *purchasing groups* in order to take advantage of group discounts for volume sale. The different forms of supply-chains require that the business understand the way that, this may *affect* your business. Successfully navigating along the path through the supply chain is essential in order to reach the customer with both product/service and with the proper message in an efficient and appropriate manner. Medical and dental services have been similarly combined, with physicians and dentists joining HMOs and forming groups and corporative entities to provide a range of services. This method provides service entities a means to enter into volume purchases of required items for their practices in a cost efficient manner, which is not available to a single practice.

Chapter 20- Qualitative Measures

The previous Chapters of Part III focused upon the implementation steps involved in accomplishing the development of business.

This Chapter will discuss those activities that are important qualitative and quantitative measures involved in an enterprise such as discovering the *Value of Intangibles*.

"Data"

The selection of the right people to do a job is one of the most significant actions that a business will make. It is important that the choices made be thorough and accurate. There are few direct measures to apply in any job position other than perhaps sales and profit however, it is necessary that the most capable individual, be selected for the position. The first part of the process requires a description of the position and the responsibilities involved during the performance of the role. Developing the talents of the staff and support personnel represents an investment and as with other investments, it is important that progress be "*tracked*", and return-on-investment evaluated periodically.

That is not a precise *science* however, through establishing of goals and objectives, a quantitative and qualitative assessment is possible to determine where strengths and weaknesses lie, and appropriate counseling provided. This is but one of a number of intangibles that have an impact on the successful development of an enterprise. The remaining chapters in this Part will explore these identified areas.

The 'Wealth Of' Business Enterprise

To explain the marketplace, Adam Smith penned "A WEALTH OF NATIONS" [3]. This seminal work set the stage for the thinkers of the 250 years that followed to expand upon and to apply, as the industrial revolution unfolded. It led to a fundamental understanding of the free enterprise system and the refutation of Mercantilism, hence was a framework that subsequently lead to the individual freedom and property rights that we enjoy today.

The significant value of Adam Smith's principle has application today to current business enterprise.

The lesson of the individuals in the *free market* determining the value and quantity of product voted upon by individuals exercising their preferences by exchange of their money, for the value that the seller places upon his product is in play during every free transaction made in the market throughout the world. This *invisible hand* [3] has application directly to the resource called human talent. One of the major factors involved in the wealth of business enterprise is at play in the acquisition and development of human talent. Complementary to the development of talent is the evaluation and utilization of talent currently employed by the enterprise.

Anecdote: Training and developing personnel

It is important to look toward the potential of individuals not only in the near term, but also in their and the organizations future.

During a meeting with the owner of the company, we were discussing a number of employee's performance, and potential, it became clear that a few individuals were exhibiting exemplary performance. The discussion led to a question of these employees capability to accept future additional responsibilities. There were two individuals in particular who stood out. One was an engineer, who was rather low key, but exhibited innovative capability. The second was an individual who did not have an extensive educational background but exhibited a great deal of enthusiasm, motivation and talent. As time went on, changes took place in the business and some people were no longer with the company.

The two aforementioned employees were candidates for promotion to management positions. A review of their performance by management showed that their performance was excellent. The engineer however was difficult to motivate and was prone to procrastination. The other person was always looking at ways to move the company forward in his area of responsibility and beyond.

He was less formally educated but was ambitious and motivated. When a position in management became vacant, he volunteered to take over this area, and learn on the job, as well as continuing his responsibilities, and completing his high school education. He succeeded in accomplishing both activities. Two years later, he had achieved an extensive understanding of problem solving methods, was actively engaged in solving problems using innovative methods. He helped the company achieve significant improvements in goals and objectives and in motivating people. He then took on a role of administrating a number of Operations Management programs, when the position became available, and succeeded in achieving

> *a restructuring of the manufacturing organization that increased production and reduced costs.*
>
> *The company was successful and sold to a suitor, in part a result of his accomplishment. He is now in charge of the operation.*

During the early stages of an enterprise development, the organization is typically composed of a President and a Secretary/Treasurer, the minimum requirement for Incorporation as a Company or business entity. The company progresses to a level where a need for change in the company organization may be clear for further company growth. When change becomes necessary in positions of authority, responsibility and accountability, for accomplishing the goals and objectives of the organization, it requires that re-structuring take place within the company.

"A change of structure"

Originally, what was a two-person organization can no longer do the job required as the business structure is no longer able to meet the expanded requirements. This become evident when the business requires that the Entrepreneur/President / Principal in the business can no longer control the *running* of the business through management of the mundane day-to-day activities. The Entrepreneur may spend time looking at the advances that need to take place for future growth in product/ service and concentrate on bringing in the resources to accomplish the plan.

Under these circumstances, companies often seek management recruiters to obtain candidates for the Management of the Business, a *Business Manager*.

The hiring of a business manager means that the company may then be in a better position to focus attention to the inside needs of the enterprise and separately focus on the resource needs from outside sources to accomplish future growth. It also provides the enterprise the means for looking at developing new products or pursuing product improvements by separating the managing of the *business* from focusing on the R&D and Financial needs of the organization. It also provides a path for Resource Planning as the company grows.

The business, if successful, evolves into an expanded organization structure as it grows from that of a President, Secretary/Treasurer to an organization with perhaps separate functions for a President, Chief Executive Officer//Chief Financial Officer/Chief Operations Officer, Manufacturing, Quality, Engineering, Procurement, Finance, and R&D structure.

Further growth, and the structuring for issuance of company stock on the market, will determine the structure for expansion in financial positions. For example; Chairman of the Board of Directors and Directors, President/Chief Executive Officer, Department Managers.

Anticipating these paths early in the life of the enterprise provides for sound planning of the company's growth, and developing in house personnel talent for these new positions to be able to make these transitions smoothly and timely

An Analogy: Poker and Business

In the poker game 'Texas Hold Em' the dynamics of a business is played out. Each player's finances are at stake with every turn and hand. In this game, each player determines the chances for their success, and the dynamics of the market (risk/reward). The player's choices are dependent upon a number of factors with each card turned and with the betting of each player in the pot. Risk assessment takes place prior to each move and there are intangibles present with every bet or fold of a hand. The Poker game continues until there is a winner. The extent of the financial gain or loss is dependent upon the skill and experience of the player, the player's ability to assess the competition and the management of resources. In this manner, the comparison exists to an enterprise. In an enterprise, the business finances are at risk with decisions on expenditure and introduction and offer of the product/service in the marketplace. The resultant choices are dependent upon a number of factors with each major decision taken. An assessment of ongoing risk takes place for each of the variables. In business, gain or loss is determined against the financial risk and expenditure and stated in the Business Statements of P/L and Operating Expenses. The reward or winning is determined upon completion of monthly transactions.

Existing Versus Growing

The purpose of an enterprise is to grow, not to just exist. In order to provide the tools to accomplish growth requires assessing the direction and purpose of planned growth. Companies often will approach the future without the benefit of visibility due to the lack of input and the rate at which changes are taking place in their respective field.

It is important that an organization identify the goals and objectives for accomplishing sustained growth. It is important that the business plan reflect the best estimate of the growth curve with intervals where assessment of progress made, and results achieved. The window of visibility should be more than *now* and *five years* from now, and programs put in place to achieve the plan. The growth of an enterprise is not static it is dynamic hence when goals and objectives are defined and programs are put in place in order to achieve the defined endpoints, frequent reviews and analyses must be made. The endpoints should be both realistic and consistent with resource planning and financial objectives.

Using the Senses

The term *gut feel* does not always refer to indigestion, although that may be *valid* in the business world environment. Our *senses* provide a valuable tool in assessing the *feeling* about events and people, and explored as a positive input to the more *formal* assessment by *analytical* means. The *grasp* of a problem is an effective means to describe the scope of an issue. It is necessary to define a problem in its full context prior to determining a means to resolve the issue.

Anecdote 4 Potential Talent

Always ask a person applying for an engineering related position if they carry a 'pocket knife'.

During an interviewing of people for engineering and technician related positions for a company, those individuals who responded to the question affirmatively were 'tinkerers' the kind of talent that is necessary for creative work.

Similarly when reviewing candidates for analytical or

> computer related positions I found that those people
> who were engaged in software games and other 'nerdy'
> hobbies possessed the type of learned habits that can be
> utilized in application roles.

In the *business world,* it is often necessary to take a step back in order to see what is going on. A solution to the *wrong* problem will not resolve the issue at hand. Use of the senses provides additional input. Along with objective measure, reality is the *perception* of an issue. To illustrate how the senses are important fact gathering, observe the following situation.

During early aerospace experience, an astronaut was orbiting the earth in a Space Capsule while talking to the Spaceflight Center in Houston, Texas. The technician noticed that the astronaut's *heart rate* was unexpectedly rising as he was speaking with him. He asked the astronaut if he was in distress. The astronaut responded that he was all right. The technician noticed that the astronaut's voice was a little *tense.* He then asked the astronaut what he was doing. The astronaut said that he was just trying to look out the window of the spacecraft. The technician asked him what he was observing. The astronaut responded, "right now I can't see anything my *helmet's* visor is all FOGGED UP!"

The Qualitative Aspect of Progress

Progress may be determined through measures that have been established and monitored. Progress may also be determined through subjective or *qualitative* aspects that fill in the picture of the *wellbeing* of the enterprise.

An event took many years ago while managing at a company. Rumor had it that there was going to be a layoff. A management meeting took place the following week, to discuss among other matters the changes that have taken place in the market and where we were with respect to change in the workforce.

The rumor mill had learned of the meeting, before there was any consideration given to having a layoff, and based upon *their* assessment of where the business was headed, had raised the likelihood of this happening. The unofficial communication system is an effective way of gauging sentiment and attitude of the workforce.

Managing Risk

There are times in business, as well as other aspects of life, where critical errors are committed and mistakes occur. It is important to remember that mistakes *will* occur. It is necessary to develop the ability to separate the factual events from the emotional aspect of the events. When confronted with a problem resulting from individual action or inaction, the acknowledgement of the mistake and taking responsibility for the situation is the single most important item on the road to appropriately handing the outcome.

"History and action"

Severe threats to safety and survival confronted primitive humans. The people responded to these challenges by acting through the flight or fight reflex. It was not a *reasoned response to stimulus* it was the *primitive* brain that controlled action.

Since then we have also developed a *reasoning* brain where we take the time to think through our response to danger or damage, however, we frequently encounter the *false alternative* condition or choice. When asked "which would you prefer loosing, your left arm or right leg", approximately 7 in 10 people would respond with a choice of one or the other. The question is *"biased"* toward making a choice response.

The rational answer is *neither.*

In a similar manner when a problem occurs it is all too often *easier* to respond by either impulse or impotence, that is by either taking rapid action without proper thought or analysis, or by avoiding it altogether. If a manager or executive of a company makes the correct decision 70-90% of the time they are doing well.

There is a wide path between impulsive action and avoidance. There is a *method* for managing risk. This method involves considerations and action as follows; identification of the issue, analysis of the facts, investigation into the root cause, deciding on a course of action based upon the analysis, taking the appropriate action. This does not presuppose that there is always a *unique* solution or result to the problem, but it does provide the best opportunity to reach a reasoned action.

Risk analysis and risk management may not be a complex process. It can be an intuitive way to deal with many cases.

Consider that when an individual arises in the morning and prepares for work, drives to work, and begins working at their job, a number of *problems* that were *possible* to happen did not occur because, they were mitigated. For example, the simple acts of preparing breakfast involves potential hazards, from being burned using a stove, using a knife to cut a roll, to pouring coffee from a hot coffee maker. Then there are the hazards of driving to work, changing lanes, avoiding pedestrians crossing the street, parking in a parking lot with other autos in motion, etc. These examples illustrate that we take for granted many events and actions that require our attention and focus. The fact that we are able to traverse this dangerous set of circumstances and only rarely encounter damage to self or automobile is proof of the need and the value of risk management. This is even more significant when we act in the business environment.

Choosing paths to ends involve a process of choices. Unexpected events take place in the process. In as *simple* a case as choosing a supplier for a material or component for your production or service requires attention to detail and clarity in communicating need and the options available. In most instances, we take time to ferret out the details needed to succeed in procuring the right items and delivery on time however, this may not have happened.

Navigating the Course
"Directing the business"

Event markers established along the path enable the navigation of the course. To illustrate, an executive of a company had a little picture framed and displayed upon one of the walls in his office. The picture showed railroad tracks crossing a dessert and disappearing into the background scene. Below the picture was a caption it read; "If you don't know where you are going any road will get you there"! The point is that without defined goals and objectives there is no way to achieve or determine success in reaching the aims of the company. An enterprise should establish milestones and time-lines for accomplishing its defined goals and objectives, and needs to evaluate the progress toward achieving these aims.

Frequent review and analysis is important to provide not only a measure of success but the issues that may have occurred which will requires commitment of resources or changes to the direction being pursued. Today there are many computer application programs to make the task doable without taxing the organization. These programs can be operated and reports distributed as frequently as desired and with minimum upkeep to achieve the desired results.

A few definitive approaches in running an enterprise need understanding.

There are companies that act in an unstructured manner. The people in the company may not have job descriptions, have a defined responsibility, or work for one boss. Companies are, in their early growth, frequently run by an *entrepreneurial* leader, rather than a *business* person, who is a creative individual who structures the company so that it is reactive to events rather than acting proactively when determining the direction for the company to pursue. Some individuals perceive the establishment of a formal *structure* as *limiting options* and *stifling creativity* and *personal growth*. Nothing could be farther from the truth.

Chapter 21- Future Expectation

As a venture reaches a stage where the frantic process of growth and development yields to reasoned reflection, and new direction, it is important to identify the next phase of the enterprise. In some instances, reaching this point in time represents an event. It is important to note that the accomplishment is not just reaching an event it is the value and benefit of learning derived from the *process* along the road traveled. Going from start, as a fledgling, and traversing the landscape of the business environment with all of its pitfalls and achievements is where we encounter the *essence* of learning and growth. It is where we acquire the wealth and expand the intellect.

Working for a company that was undergoing a period of fast growth, the company was in *transition* from being lead by the *entrepreneur* to that of the *business manager* was quite interesting. During this period, a number of business *as usual* methods underwent significant *revision* and new methods, techniques and goals were established and implemented. During one management meeting, we were discussing a significant issue that affected our transfer of the new product from R&D to manufacturing and subsequent product introduction.

It was clear that a number of detours in the road had been properly resolved, as we reached the end of the program. The new manager made a statement that was profound. He said; *"These are the really important times in the progress of the program. It is while we are in the process of confronting the problems, such as we are now, that we are learning and growing as individuals and we as a company. It is the time when we are deriving a benefit that is enduring. It is when we reach the successful accomplishment of the program objectives that we are lauded, but that is only an event."*

Reaching Maturity

During the development of an enterprise, the goals change to reflect the status of the enterprise and the changes that have occurred in the market. As time progresses we sometimes lose track of the enormous learning experience we have undergone. We often reach a point in time, which is different for each enterprise, person, and field, where we reach an understanding of who, what, how, when and where we are. This revelation is a point where reflection provides an opportunity to see *how far* we have come. It is also a time to reflect on where we are on the path of the enterprises existence. Reflection occurs as a company reaches maturity, where the past is introduction to the future. It is a stage of business growth where the enterprise can see where it is and ask the question, *"What is next?"*

Planning For the Future

During the trip, the future was a nondescript point in time. At this point in the development of the enterprise, it is prudent to make plans for the future. It may seem premature to give thought to future paths. It is more significant than is often expected.

Think for the moment what could be more important to the enterprise than to look at how we are going to proceed to the next phase of the organization. Who is capable in taking the enterprise the next step, is there a succession order, are individuals identified, have they been trained. Is the sale of the enterprise a viable path, and if so, have the financial factors been explored.

There is another interesting consideration. During the growth and development of the enterprise, which may have taken years or decades, relationships with individuals has made it possible to accomplish the achievements. These individuals are an extended family in that they have contributed, been there when the going has been rough, provided the energy and enthusiasm beyond the call of duty. These individuals are and have been important to arriving at where the enterprise is today. Therefore, some business people see this as a moral responsibility to provide the basis for continuing the enterprise, rather than selling the business to strangers who did not develop the culture that exists now. These questions require discussion and exploration.

In today's market, venture capital firms and other enterprises are constantly seeking out successful companies to acquire, expand, integrate with other companies, and to expand and secure market share. An enterprise that is open to *public* ownership has an added consideration, the stockholders as well as the stakeholders described previously. Legal, responsibilities, as well as fiducially responsibility, may require planning and action. Additionally, there is the goodwill and the legacy of the enterprise that is involved in the future transactions of the business. These factors have a bearing on value and reputation, factors that determine the worth of the enterprise.

Dealing with the Future

Now is the time to look to the future and to deal with it rather than having it happen. A distinction that applies to future direction; *you can let things happen to you, or make things happen for you*! There have been fundamental changes, in the world, which have a direct impact with the future of business enterprise. These changes have been substantive and structural. Rapid changes in transportation and communication, shifts and directional changes in demographics, as well as societal and geopolitical change may have occurred.

Global and International Systems and Methods

The business environment has changes drastically in the past century. The method for establishing acceptability of produced items during the early part of the 20th century was different from today. Individuals formed craft guilds that were the training ground for professional craftspeople and apprenticing was the method for gaining expertise in a craft. With the advent of machinery to accomplish difficult tasks, in the various industries, such as mining, oil drilling, laying rail, producing steel from iron and other *hard* industries, standardization and systematic processing ensured consistency, accuracy and interchangeability. Standards of measure, weight, and properties of materials established methods for controlling trade. Standards developed by engineers, architects, and trades people who were serving the public in such endeavors as food, feed, and trading became the basis for acceptance. Federal and Local agencies responding to health safety and potential fraud led to the promulgation of standards and requirements imposed upon the industries serving the public.

The *inventive* and *innovative* expansion that took place during the 20th Century resulted in the creation of new items of ever increasing complexity.

This had a result of potential higher risk products of all kinds. The primary concern dealt with potential safety issues arising from electrical products, appliances and health care products and services. Private organizations began to appear, to provide a means for testing and assuring control of risk of fire, shock, or damage from faulty designed or built product. One such organization was UL-Underwriters Laboratory. The UL as the name implies, was for the purpose of testing and assuring the safety of materials and devices that had a potential risk of fire and shock hazard. The qualification *called listing of an electrical product* by UL is a method for assessing and defining risk, and still provides a service to insurance companies who sell insurance to companies and producers or manufacturers of potential risk devices or materials.

The United States Pharmacopeia establishes definitive sets of rules, tests, and criteria for chemicals, biologicals, and pharmaceuticals as a means for standardization and demonstration of suitability of safety and consistency.

The establishment and implementation of Systems and Methods provide the basis for evaluating and controlling the advertised and risk aspects of products shipped worldwide. In order to accomplish this on a wide scope, such as in diverse cultures or third world countries and industrial countries, as well as the scope of multiple language and stages of development, Global standardization is in process of being developed, and implemented.

The International Standards Organization (ISO) coordinates and publishes these activities. The purpose is to provide a uniform set of *standards* for use throughout the world. The organization has a *task force* consisting of technical experts from around the world who draft standards that codify requirements for systems and products. The ISO had initially drafted a Quality document ISO9000 that provided the ground rules and methods for judging Quality Systems used in a wide range of products, services, and private and public organizations. This effort has expanded significantly from its initial charter. It now covers many products and services in international trade.

In addition, the European Union, the United States, Canada, Australia, New Zealand, Japan, China, and other countries throughout the world have adopted ISO standards, have instituted their own specific requirement in a number of specialty fields, or have formed groups to pursue unique applications. One such organization is the Global Harmonization Task Force (GHTF). This organization is currently generating standards for use in the Medical Device field. This effort will result in a *uniform* set of standards and requirements and methods for *worldwide* Manufacturing, Design Control and Testing of devices in order to assure that *all* countries use the same criteria in assuring that medical products are designed, and manufactured, under controlled conditions.

In other areas, changes over the past century have necessitated establishing systems and controls due to the expansion of technological breakthroughs as well as necessity to deal with fast changes in the world economy and culture. The following illustrates some of these changes and their impact.

During the early 20th Century transporting food, product, and people, was by horse drawn carriage, rail, barges plying rivers and ships or vessels Communication was through the newly developed telephone/telegraph systems, by *post*, or by courier. This meant that the cost of transporting perishable goods such as farm product, and cattle limited the potential for expansion of those industries. Shipping and delivery costs and time added to the cost of goods sold, and tariffs were carefully determined.

Transportation costs was based upon the weight or size of the products, most fresh food products including fruits and vegetables as well as dairy product that sold to and purchased from local groceries were burdened with these costs. Cattle were grown butchered and then shipped to local meat markets for sale to the public. Only fish from adjacent lakes and stream or from the ocean in those areas adjacent to the Gulf or the Atlantic and Pacific Oceans were available.

The advent of the automobile and trucking industry, as well as the aircraft and extended range fast moving trains and ships, made it possible for goods to *ship* to locations previously prohibited. Products were on sale in all 48 contiguous United States, under the jurisdiction of the Interstate Commerce Commission (ICC). Modern Merchant Vessels were able to deliver goods to foreign countries less expensively and sooner, through foreign ports

A result of the expansion of shipping of product was the establishment of international requirements. The United States Department of Commerce, along with the Federal Trade Commission, promulgated requirements for Trade and Tariffs rules, for goods Exported/Imported into the United States through control and issuance of export/import licenses. The transportation and importing/exporting of products between countries has changed where the focus is now on the trade between both countries, and trading groups/blocks/regions/partnerships.

The European Union, Asian, South American and the other Latin American and Caribbean countries established mutual trade treaties, codified in agreements known by the initials NAFTA, CAFTA, ASEAN, EU have come into being for the expressed purpose of providing *Free Trade* between countries and economic groups. The establishment of the World Trade Organization, (WTO), the World Bank, International Monetary Fund (IMF) and Organization for Economic and Communication Development (OECD), etc. has encouraged provided data and expanded the range of trade, to a Global scope.

"Global markets"

These changes have had a significant impact upon the *conduct* that business is required to meet. It has had a significant impact upon; how in the past, now in the present, and how in the future business will be conducted in the world. The costs of doing business in this environment will need to consider local, national and international competition and markets.

It will no longer be selling to a market limited in size

and scope, but must also consider the cost and price of product or service based upon current labor and material cost throughout the world. Competition requires that given the same product quality, reliability, durability, the *least* expensive labor/material cost will prevail. An example of a service industry that recognized this principle within the last decade is the customer service activity developed in India, the Philippines, Ireland and other countries, where English is spoken which has provided a cost advantage to computer/software companies. Providing less expensive labor made it possible to provide service 24/7 due to the economy of service at the geographic locations of these countries.

Enterprise considering and planning to enter the marketplace in this environment, must be prepared to do business differently than that which had been developed over the past half century in the United States. The imperative is to understand the opportunities and challenges of engaging in a Global trade and economic environment. It requires both education and training in the cultural aspects of the market and the regulatory requirements of the marketplace. Furthermore, the *business plan* must contain a forward-looking analysis and planning for the anticipated *Global market*.

Improving Efficiency- Doing More with Less

Efficiency of a business is a comparison of the *input versus output*. The cost of labor is a major cost in producing commodities or product, in many industries, hence reducing labor cost or increasing output would result in greater efficiency. This reduced price for equivalent product provides a competitive advantage and an increase in profitability. In the service industries, this model is also valid when cost of ancillary services is considered.

For example, the cost of office labor, insurance compliance and accounting labor are major costs in running a Medical Office where improving efficiency may be described as, *doing more for less*. An increase in efficiency can reduce labor cost resulting from better manufacturing techniques, improved or new equipment to do the job, or job simplification through training.

Using Technology to Improve Efficiency

Prior to the middle of the twentieth century data was entered into ledgers manually, on cards, or on paper. Adding machines and comptometers were early ways to perform data entry and analysis. It was a time consuming process subject to human error. With the advent of calculators, punch cards and computers, data entry and data analysis significantly improved business efficiency.

The early computers were simple devices but expensive in cost. The huge mainframe computers use was for accounting activities, namely the storage and crunching of data. The software was simple, but not necessarily easy to use and consumed vast amount of energy to develop. The need for more advanced software attracted people, many of who were viewed as strange and referred to, in an unflattering manner, such as egg- heads, nerds or geeks because that had unusual appearance and creative talent.

In the early 1980's a major change took place in computer technology, the development of the Personal Computer or PC. IBM was the first company to pioneer this development and entered into a contract with a startup company for developing an Operating System (OS) for use as the computer system software. This startup company was Microsoft. Microsoft developed an 'OS' Operating System which was called PC DOS that was designed to work on the IBM PC. Microsoft retained rights to the software concept and when the contract with IBM was completed, Microsoft created a version of the OS called Microsoft MS DOS, which was the fundamental operating system that expanded the use of computers, even today.

The advent of the PC and subsequent computer innovations made it possible for businesses and individuals to perform tasks that were not capable of performance prior to that time. It enabled conducting complex tasks that previously required vast numbers of people and long amounts of time, to accomplish with fewer people and in a smaller amount of time to complete.

The PC with its OS created not only a single line of product and its complementing software. It spawned a *robust industry* that made possible vast improvements in efficiency and applications that were not available previously. This one event, the development of the PC and the Operating System, has done more toward expanding the sphere of capability of human endeavor than almost any other technology prior to its inception or subsequently. It has also made space exploration, more accurate weather forecasting, worldwide information and personal communication amongst individuals and business, and all manner of devices and equipment possible. There is no end in sight. Doing *more with less* has been a steady path started by invention and innovation and progressing beyond the most farsighted ideas.

CHAPTER 22- EXPANSION

Organizations reach a point in their development where they may seek to expand by introducing other products or services. The motivational factors involving product development or expansion is often through obsolescence of existing product or innovation in the market, acquiring additional resources in developing new product, or the need to expand into other areas of service or technology. Expansion may mean seeking either similar companies in the industry or companies that can complement your product line. It is less expensive to utilize an existing marketing and sales force to market two or three products, than it is to establish separate functions for each product.

There are opportunities for merging with other companies in order to provide resources which can be made available and create a realm where the merging companies are greater than the sum.

Acquisition

When a company or service organization is successful, the principal(s) may see an opportunity to acquire another entity to supplement or augment the existing company level of activity. It is common to see organizations develop a structure through other entities or Divisions, through acquisition. This often provides an advantage of forming a conglomerate or integrated business profile. Examples include companies such as Textron, Colgate, Kimberly-Clark, and many of the companies listed on the Stock Exchanges throughout the world.

There may reach a time when the principal(s) look toward selling the business as a means of obtaining financial independence, or for retirement.

A successful company may provide an opportunity and advantage to a buyer where the buyer may want to accomplish growth or diversification of product through the acquisition of a company.

This may be pursued through brokers or agents who have an existing base of companies or; who may be interested in acquiring the company, an existing company who wishes to expand capability, increase the number of customers, expand the product available to market, or to complement the business model without having to expand through only internal growth.

Defining Success

The sum total of nature, nurture, experience and learning comprise wisdom. It usually does not occur early in life, nor does it automatically appear. It is achieved through the synthesis of diverse and seemingly unrelated conditions and events that have relevance and meaning to ones existence and have taken place within the sphere of an individual awareness. The value of this achievement is unique to each individual. If it is a shared achievement with other people, it may be the best test of significance of each of our experiences in life. Sharing with others accumulated knowledge that one has learned is the hallmark of wisdom and can be a legacy and a vibrant expression of the culture.

Sir Isaac Newton is purported to have said, when asked how he was able to discover so much during his life; "If I have seen further than others it is because I have stood on the shoulders of giants". We all share that legacy.

CHARTS AND FIGURES

Figure-A- Number of Businesses in the U.S.

SBA Summary Statistics for Small and Large Business Measures

Variable	1988 Mean	2002 Mean
Small Business Firms	103,106	118,851
Small Business Establishments	110,171	127,354
Small Business Employment	987,171	1,162,183
Small Business Payroll	18,600,000	36,600,000
Small Business Births	12,711	13,999
Small Business Deaths	11,638	13,350
Large Business Firms	1,684	2,287
Large Business Establishments	13,883	21,216
Large Business Employment	823,646	1,157,158
Large Business Payroll	19,700,000	44,700,000
Large Business Births	1,325	2,242
Large Business Deaths	1,005	2,064

Note: For this table, small businesses are those with fewer than 500 employees and large businesses are all others.

Birth and death data are for 1989 and 2001

Figure B- Percentage of Small Business-Number of Employees

Small Business Compared with Total Business Activity

Variable	2002
Total Business Firms	121,138
Total Business Establishments	148,570
Total Business Employment	2,319,341
Total Business Payroll	81,300.000
Total Business Births	16,241
Total Business Deaths	15,414

Small Business

Small Business Firms as a % of total	98
Small Business Establishments % of total	86
Small Business Employment % of total	50
Small Business Payroll % of total	45
Small Business Births (starts) as % of total	86
Small Business Deaths (failures) as % of total	87

Conclusion:

- **Small firms represent 98% of ALL firms**
- **Small business represent 86% of all establishments**
- **Small business employ 50% of all employees**
- **Small business represent 45% of all payroll**
- **Small business represent approx. 86% of all business starts, and failures in the year 2002**

Figure C- The Human Growth Curve

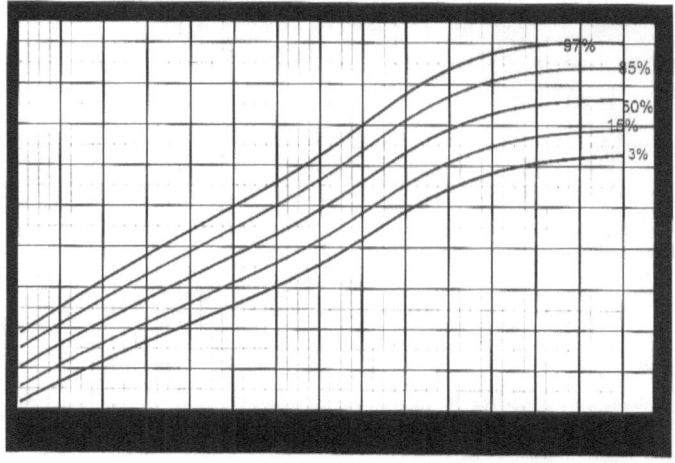

AGE ------->

Figure-D- The Failure Density Curve

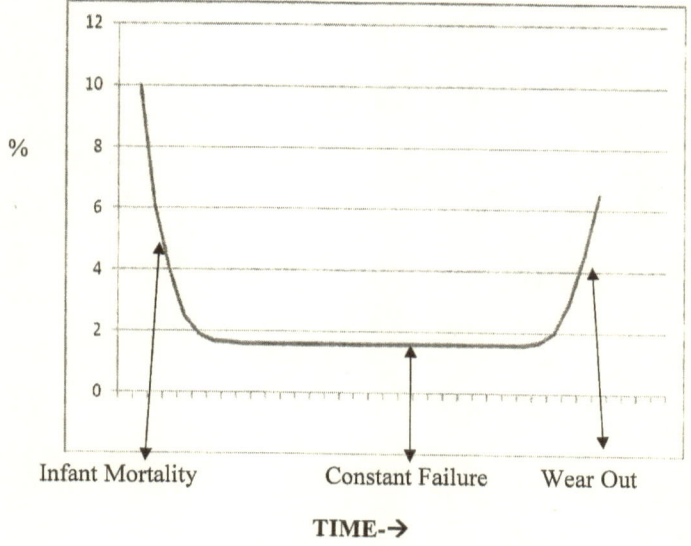

TABLES

Table 1 Balance Sheet

Assets		Liabilities & Equity	
CURRENT ASSETS	**x100**	**CURRENT LIABILITIES**	**x100**
Cash in Banks	$1000	Notes Payable-To Banks	$ 3500
Cash on Hand	$2000	Notes Payable-To Trade	$1000
TOTAL CASH	*$3000*	Notes Payable-To Other	$ 500
RECEIVABLES		Accounts Payable	$2500
Notes-Trade	$5000	Loan on Life Insurance	$ 0
Notes-Other	$1000	Due to Officer, Partners,.	$ 0
Accounts-Other	$ 300	Income Taxes Payable	$ 150
Less Debt Reserves	$ 0	Other Taxes Payable	$ 0
		Salaries & Wages Accrued	$ 600
Total Receivables-	*$9,500*	Position of Long Term Debt	$ 100
		TOTAL CURRENT LIABILITIES	*$ 8,350*
INVENTORY			
Finished Merchandise	$ 1500	*LONG TERM LIABILITIES*	
Work in Process	$ 3000	Bonded Debt	$ 0
Raw Materials	$5000	Mortgages & Leans Payable	$30000
Supplies	$1000	Notes-Long Term	$ 4500
Other	$ 500	Less Current Position	$ 0
TOTAL INVENTORY	*$11,000*	*TOTAL L-T LIABILITY*	*$34,150*
Life Insurance Surrender Value	$1000		

Government Security	$ 250		
Other Marketable Securities	$ 50		
Other Current Assets	$ 0		
TOTAL CURRENT ASSETS	***$21,800***		
FIXED ASSETS			
Land	$10000		
Buildings	$25000		
Machinery & Equipment	$ 5000		
Vehicles	$ 2500		
OTHER FIXED ASSETS			
Define	$ 0		
Sub Total			
Less Accumulated	($ 0)		
TOTAL ASSETS	***$42,500***	***TOTAL LIABILITIES***	***$42,500***

Table 2 Profit and Loss Statement

INCOME
Income	**$200,000**
Total Income	**$200,000**

Expense
Accounting	$ 3,500
Marketing & Ads	$105,000
Taxes	$ 57,000
Telephone	$ 4,800
Total Expense	$170,300

NET INCOME $ 29,700

Table 3 Retained Earnings

Assets		Liabilities & Owner Equity	
Cash	$ 6,600	Notes Payable	$ 0
Accounts Receivable	$ 6,200	Accounts Payable	$ 30,000
		Total Liabilities	$ 30,000
Tools & Equip	$25,000	Owner's Equity	
		Capital Stock	$ 7,000
		Retained Earnings	$ 800
		Total Owners Equity	$ 7,800
TOTAL	$ 37,800	TOTAL	$ 37,800

Table 4 Statement of Cash Flow

CASH FLOW

Statement of Cash Flow for the period 01/01/2006 to 12/31/2006

Cash flow from operations	*$ 4,000*
Cash flow from investing	*$(1,000)*
Cash flow from financing	*$(2,000)*
NET INCREASE (decrease) in cash	**$1,000**

References:

1) Abraham de Moivre, "The Doctrine of Chances" (1738), and Laplace "Analytical theory of probabilities" (1812) are credited with developing the mathematical rationale for the *Normal Curve* or *Gaussian distribution,* as a basic statistical measure of natural characteristics, also called the 'Bell shaped curve'.

2) Milton Freidman, "Capitalism and Freedom" (Chicago: University of Chicago Press 1962) Chapter 1 pp 7-17. Dr. Freidman espouses the virtues of free enterprise and unrestrained competition as the formulae for economic growth.

3) Adam Smith, "The Wealth of Nations ", 1776

4) Shigeo Shingo, "Story of 'TOYOTA' Production System from Industrial Engineering Viewpoint". 1981

5) Wikipedia, "Innovation", (Wikipedia, the free encyclopedia)

ABOUT THE AUTHOR

The Author is president of Allen Hans & Associates, Incorporated (AHA) a Medical Device consulting firm that he founded in 1986 and during the past 23 years has successfully served over 30 companies and institutions

His background and experience in management and engineering positions over the past 50 years focused

on high technology components, devices and systems. During this period, he developed, directed and supported Quality System and Regulatory Compliance activities for a number of companies.

During a recent eight (8) year period, he directed the activities of a Medical Device company in Guadalajara, Mexico as 'Chief of Mexican Operations', until the company was sold.

Eight years ago, he co-developed, and currently teaches, a course in 'Quality Systems and Standards' as a part of a Masters Degree program, at USC, in Regulatory Science.

Prior to starting his consulting company, he was associated with companies that developed state of the art medical devices, such as implantable cardiac pacemakers, ambulatory vital signs monitors, and hospital patient monitoring systems.

His previous experience includes 12 years in the Aerospace industry in quality assurance systems, engineering and manufacturing Solar Cells and Solar Panels used in satellites and spacecraft.

He was for 6 years involved in Research & Development, and Quality Engineering in the Manufacturing of semiconductors.

He holds a Doctorate in Business Management from Los Angeles University and is a licensed Professional Quality Engineer in the State of California. He has authored papers and presented papers at industry seminars. He is a member of the Regulatory Affairs Professional Society (RAPS), and for 8 years had been on the Editorial Advisory Board of the Medical Device and Diagnostics Industry (MDDI) magazine.